LOOKING AHEAD

LOOKING AHEAD

How Your Dying Impacts Those Around You

Rick Bergh, M.Div., CT

Author of *Taking Notice* and *Finding Anchors*

Looking Ahead

Published by
Beacon Mount Publishing
18 West Chapman Place
Cochrane, Alberta, T4C 1J9, Canada
www.rickbergh.com

Cover design by HRM Graphics
Interior design by Jera Publishing

ISBN 978-0-9947962-7-1 (paperback)
ISBN 978-1-988082-02-8 (ePub)
ISBN 978-1-988082-07-3 (Mobi)
ISBN 978-1-988082-04-2 (audio)
ISBN 978-1-988082-10-3 (hardcover)

Author's Note
The names, details and circumstances may have been changed to protect the privacy of those mentioned in this publication.

This publication is not intended as a substitute for the advice of health care professionals or legal counsel.

Printed and bound in the United States of America.

Dedication

This book is dedicated to the life and memory of
Pamela Faye Bergh
March 1, 1961 – July 23, 2008

Acknowledgements

I'm honored to share this story. It's mostly a story about my first wife Pam with whom I shared almost 25 years of married life. The pages of this book are also interlaced with many examples of others who chose to see life in their dying and, as such, penned a closing chapter to their lives that left a significant impression on those who surrounded them. I feel honored to have known these people and been with them in their final days.

I need to thank the church that I was pastoring during that time (St. Peter's Lutheran in Cochrane, Alberta) for their amazing support and love during Pam's illness and her final chapter on this earth. They were a people of God who showed love to us every day in so many different ways.

I know we had hundreds of people praying for us during our journey. There's no way I could name them all. Being surrounded in prayer is something that is too incredible for words – we were so grateful to be sustained in that way.

Pam's mom and dad were amazing, as were her sisters, Carol Ann and Lynn, who were with us right up until Pam took her last breath.

Thanks also to our brother-in-law Scott.

My mom, sister (Carol) and brother (Dan) and all of our nieces, nephews, uncles, aunts and cousins from both sides of our family were all so good to us. I have an amazing extended family and feel very blessed. We couldn't have done it without you.

Thank you to our four children: Devon, Keeara, Larissa and Landon. It was a really tough period of time in our journey as a family, but each of you entered into something pretty amazing with your mom. You chose to be ever present and, as a result, were on the receiving end of some powerful "Mom" moments that will carry you forward forever. Your mom would be so proud of you. I love each of you so much.

I want to thank my editor, Rhonda Fleming of RJF Writing Services, for her wisdom, guidance and patience. You were a gift sent my way. I appreciate your support and belief in my work.

I want to thank my wife Erica, whom I married on July 31, 2010, in Montreal, Quebec. To have been blessed twice with wonderful wives is still beyond my comprehension. Erica is the main reason why this book has come to fruition. She is my first line editor and is able to get inside my head and understand what I want to say.

And then there is you, God. You are definitely not "way up there" nor far away from us. You are so close and desire to be near your people, comforting them. I know I yelled at you a lot during this difficult journey. I also know you wanted me to write this book. I offer these words up as an offering to you. It's all I can do. This is really a story about a woman who loved you dearly, who followed you all her life and trusted you for her next journey beyond this earth.

Pam loved you deeply and so do I.

Contents

Preface

Dying is a personal experience, but it's also a community initiative.

Your dying impacts others and could become a final gift to your family, friends and community. Although in dying you are preparing for your death, and thus living your final chapter on earth, you must not underestimate the residual effects of those final months on those close to you.

I've written this book not only for those who are terminally ill or have a life-limiting illness, but also for those who are currently living in good health. Thinking, preparing and planning for our eventual death, whether it is sudden or long-term, is not something we often consider. I believe most of us have a desire to write our final chapter well and leave the best possible footprint for our family and friends after we are no longer physically present in their lives.

This book is also for family and friends who are companioning those who are living out their last days on earth. You are being invited into an experience that may change your own life in significant ways. What part will you play in this larger story?

It's important to note that dying has life imbedded in it and should be treated as such. Because you are alive, you still have purpose. Not knowing how your final days on earth will contribute to another's future happiness, joy and direction should not keep you from inviting others into your story as it continues to unfold. It should cause you to think about how you might impact those around you in a lasting and meaningful way.

If you are terminally ill, there are some things you can do—and some things your friends and family can do as well—that will help you live out your last days to their fullest. At the same time, as you share this ongoing journey with those around you, you'll be amazed at how you can empower your family, friends and community to move forward into a new life—one that you helped shape because of your invitation for others to be part of your last days.

After years of working in this field and being with hundreds of people as they died, the most important thing I have learned is this: Dying is not just about you. While you are the focal point of the story right now, you also have much to contribute that will remain once you are gone—and would be lost forever if not shared with those whom you love. As such, your story continues with its twists and turns and also with all those whom you have chosen to be part of this chapter.

My wife Pam was diagnosed with third-stage ovarian cancer at 42 years of age. For almost five years we had shared a very significant journey together. But now reality set in as we were told by our medical team that she was no longer able to receive further treatments. We were also told the disease was progressing to the point that we needed to consider end-of-life plans.

To be honest, I am not sure if those three words—*end of life*—were the most helpful words uttered to us as we stepped into those final months of the unknown. Yes, the reality is that life on this earth comes to an end—we need to recognize that. But the finality of that phrase felt like we were forced to give in to death before life had finished with us.

For five years we had shared a very impactful journey together as a family. We had engaged in life and learned so much from living with a mom and wife with cancer. Why should dying now become an "it's all about me" event? It did not make sense to us or to Pam. So Pam chose to include her family, friends and community in perhaps one of the most intimate, significant, and vulnerable periods of her life. We knew Pam was the author of her ongoing story, but we also knew we were a big part of it as well.

If you are reading this book, you have likely been given some extra time to write the final chapter of your life on earth, with all its many uncertainties. You may want to consider these important questions:

- Who do you want to be a part of this final chapter?
- How would you like your story to unfold?
- How will your final chapter on earth be remembered?

It's time to pick up your pen and start writing. You are the author.

CHAPTER 1

When Bad News Comes, Add Yeast to the Dough

*Don't judge each day by the harvest
you reap but by the seeds that you plant.*

– ROBERT LOUIS STEVENSON

We had moved to Yellowknife, Northwest Territories, for my internship. Pam and I had just been married and were excited about our first adventure together as newlyweds. Living up north was expensive, so we immediately began to think about how we could best manage our budget. Our first cost-cutting idea? Bake our own bread!

This would be a new experience for Pam. She was so excited to take those first three loaves out of the oven. She had six more ready to go in. She removed the first batch, looked at them and said to me, "They aren't very large loaves." "It's heavy bread," I replied and added, "I like my bread like that." She seemed perplexed as she put them on the counter to cool.

Then she baked the other six loaves and set them on the counter as well. "Rick," she said, "they are not very full looking. They're really flat." "It's okay," I replied, "I'm sure they will taste great. Here, let me slice one and try it." I took out the sharpest knife we had and began to saw my way through the loaf. It was hard. So hard, in fact, that it snapped the plastic knife handle as I pressed down to cut into it. Pam started to cry. "It's okay," I said, "maybe the oven was too hot? Or maybe you missed an ingredient?" I floundered, trying to affirm her in her recent culinary attempt.

Rena, who had given us her fail-proof bread recipe, lived upstairs. So Pam asked her advice and wondered what she had done wrong. The conclusion, after investigating the options, was that the yeast was bad. It had an expiration date that we didn't notice when we bought it. The next time, the bread turned out perfectly because the yeast was good. The loaves rose and the bread tasted amazing.

Essential ingredients. What are they in your life? What do you need to include in your life right now as you enter this phase of your journey? What relationships do you need to invest in? What do you need to say? What things are on the "back burner" that now need to be brought to the forefront? These ingredients go beyond what's on your "bucket list" to the essence of who you are and how you want to be remembered. Just as yeast is intrinsic to bread, there may well be things that you need to add that are intrinsic to your dying.

In a world that seems to be increasingly self-centered, your death journey needs to take into consideration its impact on others. Working in palliative care for many years has taught me the significance of those who are willing to engage others at the end of their life on earth. These individuals recognize the wider purpose of bringing other people into their experience. The peace that comes from sharing the dying experience with a chosen community is deeply meaningful.

Dying is something you only do once, with no previous experience, so it's hard to fathom or even picture it. However, even though we don't know the future, we can be certain of one important truth: we ARE still alive. We are still breathing, still thinking, still in relationship with significant people we love. Don't lie down and give up on what life might bring to you and others, even as you near the end. That is a sure-fire way to miss out on some amazing growth opportunities that can have lasting impact.

The deep question is: What do you believe about growth and life?

Because of what you believe, have you given up on growing as a human being now that you know you're dying? Should you?

I love Hawaii. I'm always amazed at how beauty can come from a rock. Incredible hotspots under the earth's crust pushed molten lava up to the surface, and caused the formation of sea volcanoes which, over time, rose, broke the surface of the water and formed these tropical islands. Wow!

So where did this hunk of lava get its flora and fauna, especially considering the thousands of miles of ocean separating Hawaii from the nearest land? Migrating birds. Stirring currents. Howling winds. Imagine! These three elements combined to transport the seeds of various plant life to Hawaii. There the fertile volcanic soil helped nurture the growth of vast forests and grasslands. It has become known as Paradise. Who would have thought that something so beautiful could come from boiling rock?

You may feel that *you* are only a rock with little life, but you are not. You are fertile soil, still growing on the inside. What color is waiting to shine through your prism and splinter its light onto others?

- Can you see how the final chapter of your life could influence your personal growth and relationships with those close to you?
- Do you have the desire to continue contributing to the world in which you live? It might look different than it used to, but you can still breathe life into others.
- Do you want to drop seeds of wisdom that you have learned from your experience? Here is your opportunity

to communicate something that could transform someone else's life for good.

What is happening to your physical body is significant. Your body is saying, "No more—I'm done." It's becoming weaker, but your mind, spirit, heart and all of your significant relationships are still remarkably alive.

Dry yeast is like small seeds. It's a leavening agent. It's active. When combined with other ingredients, it begins to grow. When the oxygen is depleted, fermentation begins. And when the dough is baked, the yeast dies and the air pockets 'set,' giving the baked product a soft and spongy texture.

The yeast is *us* in our dying. It has a very special function and purpose.

Some of you have come to terms with the reality of your pending death. Others who are reading this have just heard the harsh news.

Pam was coming to grips with this news. She had tried so hard to beat the cancer that was eating away at her through almost five years of treatments, remission and other alternatives. It was not our job to pick up her pen and begin to write her final chapter. But I learned that she was beginning to think about her life—not by how many days she had left before she died, but by how many days she had left to live.

It's true, Pam was starting to bake bread again—literally and figuratively—a lesson she had learned many years before in Yellowknife. The significance of the right yeast did not escape her as she picked up her pen and continued to write her closing narrative.

My parents also used to bake bread together. I remember my mom and dad kneading the bread dough, often taking over for each other in the process. The combination of healthy yeast and working the dough made for great bread.

Bread is a communal experience. So is dying. Knead this experience for all it's worth. Make it what you want it to be for yourself and for others. You don't bake bread to keep it to yourself. You share it with others. So it is with the ongoing days of life until your final breath.

Your personal choices and decisions place you in the driver's seat. And although you, along with the rest of your family, will need to make important decisions along the way, this is still *your* life. But it's smart to think ahead. Especially when it comes to your ongoing purpose and contribution to those closest to you. We all need to consider the moments that are remaining with our family and friends and make the most of the minutes we spend in relationship with each one specifically. With that in mind, I would like to invite you to consider the following:

1   Why not have a conversation with the people who are closest to you? Let them know you would like your dying to be a communal and shared experience. Explain what that could mean for both them and for you.

Example: "I don't want this to be a private experience. And I don't want you to be frightened of it. There will be times when I will be anxious but also times when I will have some important things to share with you. Please enter into this experience with me. Let's share this together."

2   Which people do you want around you? Who will share those precious times with you as you look toward your last days on earth. Let them know ahead of time that you want them to be part of your story.

Example: I asked Pam who she wanted to see — other than her family — during her final days on earth. There were some very special moments shared with good friends and I am thankful we made room for those encounters. When I talked with these friends later, I learned that their conversations with Pam were significant.

3   There are certain individual family members or friends who may need a little more of your attention for a variety of reasons. Think about your contribution to that person's life. Who could benefit from extra time spent with you?

Example: I had a parishioner named John who was dying. His grandson James was struggling with alcohol. John intentionally decided to spend more time with James. The two of them had many wonderful conversations together: "He needs me more than the others," John said to me one afternoon. The time they spent together was significant in James' future following the death of his grandpa. He shared some of these important talks during the eulogy. It was powerful.

4   Think about some plans you would like to put into place. This is not necessarily in order to complete your bucket list, but to allow you to engage in those events in your life that would bring you joy in these final days.

Example: Pam's and my final trip to Hawaii, shortly before her terminal prognosis, is still one of the most beautiful memories I have of us together.

5   Depending on the illness and its limitations, think about creating special memories for those around you, ones that others can hold on to following your death.

Example: I will never forget planning out and redesigning our backyard with Pam. She knew she would never see the end result, but when I look at it now, I think about what we planned together in her last few months. It's her design and it reminds our family of her. She lives through it.

What we choose to add to our remaining time on this earth, even though we don't know how long we have, is really important. It gives us ongoing purpose. It helps us see that even in dying there is yeast that can be added to the life we live and the people we love.

It's time to get the ingredients out and bake bread, remembering to add good yeast to the dough.

CHAPTER 2

Why Your Family's GPS System Really Matters

Strength lies in differences,
not in similarities.

– STEPHEN COVEY

When the GPS product first came out for vehicles, my family quickly purchased one for me for my birthday. They believed it would keep us from getting lost. I personally did not think I had a problem.

We were heading out as a family to visit relatives who had a cottage. I had been there before, but the last time I had gotten lost, taking a wrong turn. This time, that wouldn't happen!

Maybe it's a guy thing, but as we headed out something inside of me said, "I know where I'm going!" So I turned off the GPS and set it aside. "I'll use it in case of an emergency," I justified. After all, I could figure it out by myself, thank you very much.

As we got closer to the lake, our son Devon asked if I was going to turn the GPS back on. "I don't need it," I said casually. "I know where I'm going. I know what turn to take." "Dad," said Devon, "the last time you took the wrong road." "I know," I replied, "but I'm good." I kept on driving. One of the kids piped up, "I think that was the road, Dad." "No, it's one more," I responded, confident of my navigational prowess. I kept on driving and turned onto the next gravel road. Twenty minutes later, I knew I had taken the wrong turn — again.

"Dad, why don't you just turn on the GPS?" "Fine!" I said in defeat. It led us right to the cabin. The kids were smirking in the back seat. Humbled, I said very little. But the GPS found its way to the bottom of the cupboard very quickly.

Navigating together is a huge part of dying. Your family's GPS system is important as you travel this road — together.

What is a family GPS system?

Within each family unit, there are a number of members. Each one will be different in terms of what they bring to the table in their understanding of death and dying.

This understanding is pulled out when necessary and guides each person in their relationship with the one who is dying and with all the other members of the family unit. Do you sometimes wonder why conflict and misunderstanding surface during this challenging time? It happens often. It's because we each have our own individual "GPS system" that guides us in crisis and it may be different from the next person's GPS system. Each person tries their best to manage transition, but it looks different for everyone.

What each person has come to believe about death and dying will greatly influence how those around *you* interpret, interact and contribute to this journey of dying within the family, even if you are the primary focus. It's the story inside their head and it feels true for them. Even if you are the one who is terminally ill, they may need air time to express what they are feeling as well, as crazy as that might sound.

If you are a caregiver or family member to the one who is dying, it's helpful to think about and name those influencing factors that have come to be part of your death and dying navigation system.

There are no right or wrong answers in this analysis, but there are important foundational assumptions that need to be examined, and perhaps challenged, as they can affect whether someone's passing is healthy and peaceful or not. It's good to identify your own GPS navigational system and to think how it might be similar or different from those closest to you.

As we began to think and reflect on Pam's remaining days, I could not help but consider our family's GPS system. It had become crystallized over the years and was now a melting pot of two cultures — Pam's and mine. Even though we each brought similar worldviews from our families of origin, each of our families was different — our marriage and family were a melding of backgrounds. These backgrounds included what I would refer to as cultural differences.

For example, I learned many things from Pam about the importance of touch. When I began to date her, I quickly realized that hugging was a big part of her family's background. So were the words "I love you" which she spoke often. We did this somewhat in my family of origin, but Pam's family did it all the time.

I specifically noticed this when only a short time after we started dating, Pam's grandpa died and the manner in which she openly expressed her emotions was beautiful and healthy. We spent many hours talking about her grandpa whom she loved deeply. We cried together, held each other close and entered into this experience from her cultural background. "I love you" and big hugs are engrained in the way that the Bergh's "do life" now on a daily basis.

Our daughter Larissa used to come with me to the hospital as a four-year-old. We would visit those who were sick and dying. She wanted to come. She wasn't afraid. She would sit on the edge of the bed, softly stroke the person's arm and sing a little song. She melted the hearts of the patients.

One day Landon, the youngest in the family, asked if he could view a dead body. He had never seen one. So I called Dave at the funeral home and we went there together so Landon could see what a dead body looked like.

I know it sounds strange, but my kids were never afraid of death, cemeteries or corpses. Maybe it was because I was a pastor. There is story after story of my kids, when they were young, conducting funerals for dead fish, grasshoppers or butterflies out at the lake.

We would often visit a nursing home or extended care facility. With Pam's music role, she would lead the children in singing or bring children's choirs to visit and sing for them. It was always a given that our children would go and visit with these sometimes frail and sick people.

I have an old video of Landon driving a toy car. His sister, Keeara, asked him where he was going. He said that he was going to a funeral. "Whose funeral are you going to?" she inquired. "Daddy's!" Landon replied. Fortunately, I'm still here!

Conversations about death, dying and grief were commonplace around the kitchen table. Because I was a resident minister of a funeral home, the children saw, learned and asked questions about this important part of life.

Who would have thought this knowledge and personal understanding of death and dying would be necessary so early in their lives? They were no longer kids but young adults (aged 17, 19, 21 and 22) when the news of "we can't do any more for Pam" came to our family. Of course, we knew this meant the medical profession could no longer do anything to stop the disease. However, we knew we could do lots for Pam and she was still adding to our lives in very significant ways.

Was this easy? Absolutely not. But all of our kids and myself had established some solid foundational supports and would be forced to stand on them as we faced the reality of a beautiful mom who was dying.

Parents educate their children, whether they realize it or not. We need to examine what was taught to each of us from our own unique culture and family of origin's perspective. These influences are important ingredients that need to be recognized for their positive or negative impact on our understanding of death.

When I was growing up, nobody wanted to talk about sex. Now everybody talks about it. I think the biggest problem now is not talking openly about death, dying and grief. I believe we live in a death-phobic culture that does not want to face death, talk about it openly or allow it to be explored in a manner that has life in it. Despite the fact that we see images of a skull and crossbones as well as vampires and zombies extensively in popular culture, it only serves to distance us from the intimacy of death and the imminence of mortality.

I also believe we would rather give the work of death and dying away to professionals when most of it can and should be embraced by family members. It was not that long ago that families did this work in their homes, surrounded by significant communities that knew this person well and gave support to the entire family during the final chapter and the time following death.

What did *you* learn about the topic of death growing up in your family of origin? Did your family try to shelter you from it? Did they bring you to funerals or keep you away? Did they make it a creepy thing? A normal event? Did they talk about it or change the subject?

It is amazing to me how many individuals have not had any experience with death or dying. The older we get, of course, the more we will experience death around us, especially with the aging baby boomer population. Not being afraid of death and dying will become even more important. How did you gain your knowledge of and response to death? In some families, children are not welcomed or invited into the experience of those who are dying. Perhaps their culture excludes certain family members' participation due to belief and value systems.

Even though as a child you may not have fully participated in your family's death and dying experiences, something will have rubbed off on you that has formed your death perception. You have a distinctive navigational system that needs to be identified. All of us have a GPS system that will guide and give us direction as we travel on this road with our loved one.

I was the chaplain on call when a family asked me to come and do the last rites. The Catholic husband had married a First Nations woman. I tried to be very respectful of this family as I arrived in my clergy collar with my communion set. They sat quietly as I prayed with this man, administering the sacrament. It was not their cultural background. I finished and the wife asked me to stay as one of the elders in the room began their traditional smudge ceremony. I stood in the corner, respectfully watching and praying for each of the family members.

This was a prime example of a cultural difference in one family in regard to religious preference. Can you imagine the disruption this would have caused if one or the other had interfered with their way of doing religion at the end of life on earth? Each family has its own guiding values–or GPS–that need to be considered, especially in dying.

There are many areas that are important to consider in your death and dying education formation. From a very practical perspective, you may want to reflect on the areas found below. These nine questions will help you discern what the family dynamics are and the effects they are having.

You may think these specific details are not important, but they are. Why? Because they lead to conversation. Open conversation leads to engagement. Engagement leads to discussion. Discussion can lead to involvement... and that's exactly what you want. Everyone who is important to the dying person needs to continue to participate in that person's life and add to the unfolding story. And as long as the person is alive, the story is still being written.

We must be careful not to dismiss another's perspective that might be different from our own. It's easy to judge someone else's 'take' on a situation or their contribution, but you might inadvertently shut them down if you are not careful.

When you finish looking at the questions below, be brave and honest. Sit down with each other and talk about what you could be doing differently.

1. Who is the primary communicator in the family?

In every family there tends to be one person who is the family communicator — the gatherer and disseminator of information, the broadcasting hub for family members. I'll wager that you already have that person in mind as you read this! This person might well become the advocate with the medical team and may also be the person counted on to communicate with other family members and friends or with those who are geographically separated. What person will be sharing the latest updates on behalf of the one dying? Who decides what gets communicated?

2. How have emotions and feelings been expressed in the past in the family?

The expression and openness to share one's ongoing feelings is a crucial part of death and dying. In the past, how were feelings received in similar circumstances? Will each person's feelings be acknowledged now? What happens when a harmful or negative emotion is expressed in an unhealthy way? Will you have a plan to deal with this disruption when it comes? It will happen. That's one thing that 28 years of dealing with the dying has taught me.

If you have a family history of how emotions were "done" in the past, you may want to consider tweaking those patterns if they're not working for you. Talk about this together.

3. Who will be designated to make important end-of-life decisions on behalf of the dying person?

Decisions need to be made along the way. Identify and name those who are to make the decisions and communicate them to the rest of the family. We will talk in a later chapter about what specific significant decisions will need to be firmed up in order to allow for final wishes to be honored.

4. Who will be the primary caregiver(s) in the final days?

As a person gets weaker, there will be need for more focused care from outside the medical team. Who, from outside the close family unit, will be invited to be part of the last days or even hours? Are there certain friends or members of communities that you want to be present during these closing paragraphs of your life? You need to let your family know who these will be and why. Some cultures are very restrictive even on who in the family will be present during the last moments of life. Talk about this and be clear so there is no confusion.

5. What is each family member's experience with the larger healthcare system?

What is the family feeling toward the larger healthcare systems, especially with doctors, hospitals, treatments, as well as palliative care and hospice? A difficult past experience or a favorable one can influence the decision by family members and patient. Identify these influencing factors and be honest with each other.

6. What is the place of religion at the end of life and how might differences be respected?

What has been the traditional role of religion in the family of origin? What place has religion played in past experiences? What is the dying person's view of God and the afterlife? What about family or friends? Let's get this out in the open at the very beginning.

7. What are the historical and cultural influences of the family that need to be honored?

How tight is the family unit? Do they have a history of being together during good and bad times? Is there a patriarchal or matriarchal structure that needs to be considered? Is the family separated by distance or by past conflict? Are there rituals or traditions that need to be respected? What will be the role of the larger extended family at the end of life?

8. Who is expected to be present at death?

Are there expectations of who will be there at the time of death that need to be discussed? Is there a past history of people who should or shouldn't be present? Are there certain people that you want near you in your last days?

9. How much advance care planning has taken place? Are there areas that still need to be covered?

Who can talk openly about the practical application of Directives, Power of Attorney, Wills, funeral, organ donations? Do you have a family that talks openly or do they avoid by keeping silent?

Dying really is a family affair. But a family unit involves a complex set of people. Taking a few moments to understand yourself and others, especially when it comes to each person's unique perspectives around dying, is crucial in the quest for open and honest communication. This could prevent a lot of potential challenges in the future and pave the way for a more peaceful passing as families begin to work together and not independently.

Each person should evaluate for themselves what they believe about this event called *dying*: why it might be different from another's and how to best interact with the person dying. This is just good preventative work that all families should commit to as soon as possible.

Why not start this journey by discovering your family's GPS system? Learn together how you will navigate and arrive at the same place, or at least try the best you can to be on the same page, as you honor your loved one's remaining days on earth.

CHAPTER 3
Meeting Your Passengers' Needs From the Beginning

A man's dying is more his survivor's affair than his own.

– THOMAS MANN

We had taken off in the small Cessna 185 airplane. It was winter. It was cold. We would be fine. We needed to fly into a small village in the Northwest Territories, north of Yellowknife, in the far north of Canada's Arctic. Lee was a missionary pilot and I was an intern pastor in Yellowknife. He was my supervisor.

The flight went well as we chatted and enjoyed the beauty of the land below us and the peaceful feeling of being up in the sky, in total tranquility. And then, all of a sudden, the clouds rolled in. We were socked in and could not see a single thing in front of us, below us or beside us. I was scared. Lee noticed my angst and said, "We can trust the instruments." That was hard for me to believe, considering we could not see anything outside the plane.

The clouds quickly became a heavy snowstorm — wet snow that began to freeze on the windows and wings of the airplane. I began to think of Pam, my wife of six months. I began to think about crashing, dying, not having children, or a future, or a career. Life stood still for a moment as I contemplated what could happen next.

What seemed like hours was only minutes—and yet in those minutes I did an amazing evaluation of my life. What had I become? Who was important to me? Where did I still want to go? Fear caused my mind to replay my whole life, as if on fast-forward, and I was not ready for life to end!

We had a few tense moments, but we eventually came out safely on the other side of the storm.

When we are dying, we are still the "pilot" of our plane, but there are also other "passengers" in our plane. These passengers are not experiencing what we are going through, but they're still sitting next to us, wondering about their place on this journey.

They are trying to live their life as best they can, while maintaining a relationship with you during this new and difficult transition. Yes, it is a transition. They are saying, "Someone is dying that I love. I know I'm supposed to take advantage of the remaining moments with this person. I know that my life will still go on."

Life does not stop for your "passengers" because you are dying. And even though you may feel like you are navigating through a storm that has engulfed you, the person coming to see you or caring for you might be navigating through an entirely different storm—one you may not be aware of—while being with you in your storm as well. So they are trying to weather two storms at once. They are willing to do this because they love you.

But you can guide them by offering wisdom, support and encouragement. You can build into their circumstance and life in an amazing way. You can invite them onto your plane, have them sit next to you as you share your thoughts and help them continue to discover what might be next for them.

People who are dying often assume they no longer have a purpose. They feel as if they are just biding their time. I would beg to differ—I believe that dying people have amazing insights that come from a deep place. These insights need to be planted into a receptive life and heart.

Three of our children were young adults and one was in the adolescence stage while their mom was dying. How their mom engaged each one of them uniquely and specifically was so significant.

Although I was not privy to their mom's conversations with each of them, I do recall some prayers she would offer up for her children late at night when she would frequently wake up with pain from the disease that was rapidly growing in her body. Her prayers focused on others, not herself. I prayed for her and she prayed for everyone else. One of her prayers was consistent in these times: her request for loving, faith-believing spouses for each of her children.

Three weeks before Pam died, Jaret, the boyfriend of our oldest daughter Keeara, asked to see us privately. He was coming up to visit Keeara for the weekend. Jaret arrived prior to Keeara coming home from her summer job. He wanted to talk to us.

Pam was lying down in bed when Jaret arrived. I had anticipated that he would be asking my permission to marry our daughter. In his tradition, this would normally only include the dad, but I thought it was only appropriate that Keeara's mom be included in this important conversation.

I brought Jaret into Pam's room that afternoon. Jaret had known Pam for many years. Pam loved Jaret. He really had become an important part of our family. Jaret was nervous. He sat down on the side of our bed. There were a few minutes of chit chat and then he said, "I want to ask permission to marry your daughter." He looked at me and then at Pam. I was silent. "Pam?" I said as I looked at her. I wanted her to speak into Jaret's life. And she did.

"You can marry my daughter only if your promise one thing," Pam said. Jaret looked and waited. "If you promise to keep Jesus at the center of your relationship, then I will say yes," Pam continued. I did not need to say anything following Pam's words. Pam had said it all. "I promise," Jaret said. "Then, yes!" Pam said. And they hugged.

I'm really glad that Jaret asked for Keeara's hand in marriage while Pam was still living—she was so happy to have experienced this joyful event. Jaret could have held off, assuming it would be too difficult for Pam or would cause her sadness, knowing she would not be able to be at the wedding. But it had the opposite effect. It added something very beautiful to her life and she added something significant to his and Keeara's lives.

Keeara had found the love of her life and it was Pam who spoke into Jaret's life that day, regarding love and marriage, as she lay dying. Later than afternoon, Keeara came into her mom's room, pointed to the ring on her finger and talked excitedly about the proposal that had taken place a few hours earlier on the banks of the Bow River, close to our home. Pam would celebrate their engagement only a few weeks prior to her death.

Those coming to visit you may be older or younger than my children were. The conversations you have will be unique with each person. They may not be contemplating a future partner, as Keeara was, but each person is trying to figure out what is next on their journey on this sweet earth. And they are trying to do this at the same time they are already thinking about not having you as part of their future.

What's most on their mind besides you dying?

What should be affirmed in this person's life that will give them confidence to face the future?

What questions should be asked that would lead to helpful discussions?

What insights might you have to help them grow in their life?

How you engage each person close to you is really important. How could you contribute to their personal growth and future? What is *their* ongoing story? How might what you say to them in these remaining days be a guiding force for them when you are no longer physically present in their lives?

I still carry with me today words that Pam spoke to me during her last days. I pull these words out at different times as I give honor to her voice in my life. Her words came from a deep place I had never been to and I needed to listen carefully.

Let me close this chapter by sharing some ways Pam engaged and helped me. She not only prepared for her final days on earth but she also empowered and equipped me for my ongoing life and future, knowing that I'd be without her to help me.

Pam was always supportive of me in my professional life. Even after she was given the "nothing more we can do" message, she would shoo me off to work. When I returned home, she would engage in work-related conversation, asking me what was new. Even though I would enter the house and immediately want to see how she was doing, she would find a way to turn it around and have a conversation about how I was doing. Pam knew that long after she died I would need to continue to work and provide for the family.

I always wanted to write a book and Pam often encouraged me in this area. Little did she know that I would be writing her story and sharing it with the world. Even writing this book, almost eight years after her death, I can feel her cheering me on.

Pam often encouraged me by saying what a wonderful husband or superb parent I was. Interestingly, she never spoke about our future dreams or plans together nor the fact that she would not be able to enjoy grandchildren. She was on a different journey and her faith guided her into a new hope beyond this earth.

Whether she knew it or not, she was helping me recognize and transition well into the next chapter of my life as she considered where I might "be" following her death. She truly was focusing on my needs first. Even today, I hold those conversations close as I continue to live my life to the fullest—still honoring the gift Pam was to me and our family.

When someone is terminally ill, there is a tension—like an elastic band being stretched –between the person dying and each family member. Life wants to go on. It needs to go on. It's how we are made. Where each person is in his or her life cycle will determine how we manage this tension. The one dying can actually help release part of this tension by understanding and recognizing the needs of each person who comes and converses.

When you are on a plane, the safety instructions include the use of the oxygen mask in case of emergency. They are very clear. If you are travelling with a child or a dependent person, you put your own mask on first. Then you can help them put their mask on.

As a dying person, you can give oxygen to those who come into your life, a breath of fresh air when they need it the most. You are in a position to engage people around you in a powerful and lasting manner.

It's your turn to think about the people close to you. Who will be the passengers on your journey? Consider how you can best serve them to help them continue to grow as human beings. You have a purpose…a big purpose. Make a list of these individuals and answer the questions below.

- How old are they?
- What are the biggest decisions they are making right now?
- What might be their biggest challenges?
- What questions would you like to ask them?
- How would you like to affirm them in their current situation and next steps?
- What information would you be willing to share with them from your experience?

Your life has meaning and purpose. The conversations you have with your family and friends can have a lasting impact. The very fact that you are entering into this newly discovered "vocation" will give you new direction and fulfillment. Your life is not over yet. You need to see yourself as valuable and significant to those around you—those whom you love deeply and who care about you.

Keep writing your chapter, remembering that you have some passengers with you.

CHAPTER 4

Exchanging Words Your Way

*When you don't talk, there's a lot of stuff
that ends up not getting said.*

– CATHERINE GILBERT MURDOCK

I have discovered in my life that not everyone communicates like I do. So if I want authentic and deep relationships, I must understand some of these differences and honor them.

Have you ever been frustrated because you have not been heard? Have you ever tried to share something with another person or in a group but were never given the opportunity?

Because of this, you may have left feeling upset with specific people who seemed to dominate the conversation so you decided not to spend time with them in the future.

Everyone needs the opportunity to share what is in their heart and on their mind. Without this exchange, there is no relationship of significance between two people.

How people choose to communicate with us during our final chapter can have a positive or negative impact on our ongoing story. How we communicate with others can also influence the unfolding story.

People want to share what's going on inside their hearts, but are never quite sure how to do that or when it's appropriate when a loved one is dying. "Is it selfish to talk about my feelings?" I am asked frequently in private, outside the hospital room.

People do have questions, but aren't sure when to ask them. They have feelings, but wonder when to share them. And they have thoughts, but are uncertain of their importance.

It's fair to share what's going on for you, but be aware how it might be received. Not everyone communicates the same way, so your willingness to share may not have the desired effect you had hoped for.

Would it be helpful to know...

- whether the person dying prefers to have people around them or to spend time alone, choosing only a few close family or friends when necessary?
- whether the person dying is more likely to take in information about their situation in great detail or is not concerned about the particulars?
- if the person dying is more likely to share their feelings immediately about what is going on or if they need some time to process their feelings before talking or sharing at a later time?
- if the person dying has a list of concerns on their mind they need dealt with right away or if this person is content to let dying unfold without planning?

Pam got her energy from being alone. She needed her quiet space at times. You would think that everyone would want to be surrounded by others during their last days of life on earth. That's not always true. While Pam loved people, she also enjoyed her own space. If there were too many people around, it would sap her energy—energy she needed in order to cope with her illness. Energy that was required of her emotionally as she prepared to say goodbye to her family and friends.

Pam's personality was such that she also needed to know all the details of her illness and the various options available to her. She was all about the fine details. Her intricate chart of the various medications she was to take during the last days of her life was organized well. We knew what we had to do and we scheduled it. Doing this gave Pam peace of mind.

Pam could easily express her feelings but preferred to share what she was going through with a few people she trusted and in an environment where she was comfortable. These conversations often took place late at night in our bedroom, or by emailing her sisters, or cuddling on the couch with her children, or on the phone with her parents.

Pam also had clear day-to-day tasks that needed to be accomplished. Things needing to be done and completed "today." She worked from a to-do list. She made decisions quickly and did not need to wait around for more information to get going in life.

I am an extrovert — the person closest to Pam preferred to get his energy from being with people. I wanted to be with Pam as much as I could, but she also needed her space. At first I felt guilty leaving her alone, but she understood my needs as well. "Get going and be with your friends," she would say as she ushered me out the front door.

I don't need all the details before making a decision — in fact I hate details. I am very positive in my outlook on life and see the possibilities without needing the facts that go with it. If Pam hadn't known this part of my personality, she could have mistaken it for not caring. But she knew details were not important to me. Details, on the other hand, were very important to Pam, so I needed to honor that in her life as she went through specifics over and over.

Because of my extroverted personality, I basically shared my feelings with anyone who would listen. It has always been easy for me to share my emotions. But I soon realized that sometimes I would have to be patient with Pam as she preferred a more intimate and quiet space in order to hear what was going on in my heart. The conversations we had late in the evening as we lay in bed next to each other were amazing, deep and filled with love.

It's one thing to know the communication style of those closest to you, but what about the many others who are now coming in contact with your loved one a regular basis? Wouldn't it be helpful to let all those in your circle of influence know how your loved one prefers to communicate and ask each of them to respect that? Some in your circle of influence are capable of barging into your world and spurting out information like a water hose, leaving you to emotionally mop up what they have left behind.

There is much information that seems to be required during our dying, and sometimes it's difficult news. We need the facts. There is so much we don't know because dying is a one-time event for each of us. But the manner in which these ongoing updates are shared and received is crucial in abating fears and emotionally dealing with much of what is unknown.

We also need to be continually clearing the air with family during the dying process. The rapid fire of heightened emotions, different personalities and death create a perfect storm for misunderstandings. If words linger, they tend to find a place to lodge that is filled with anxiety and stress, until they're identified, verbalized and put to rest.

With this in mind, it's also important to be aware of those outside the family who now come into your life following a prognosis. Some of your "team players" enter into this chapter of your life because you have chosen them, while others are there because you need them — the two are not mutually exclusive of course. Either way, it's important to consider how their words and actions might impede or help you to live out your final days: either in contentment or frustration.

Terminally ill people yearn to connect effectively with family, friends and healthcare professionals. They want to tell their story as it unfolds. But each person has a unique way of taking in information, processing their day-to-day challenges, engaging those around them and inviting people into their unique experience.

If a dying person is unable to talk or share their experience in their preferred way, the process of dying can become a very lonely experience. It's like having writer's block. It's hard to continue to pen the story if those around you don't understand what you need or want.

Furthermore, if family members, friends and healthcare professionals impose their way of communicating upon a terminally ill person, he/she may quickly close up or respond in a manner that is not conducive to meaningful conversation. Your story will no longer have your voice but someone else's. That's frustrating. And it only takes one comment from one person. The way words are communicated by others and how we receive them will flavor our life.

Consider a series of concentric circles — like a target. Place the people who are in your life in those circles. The closer they are to the "target" in the middle, the closer they are to you, and their effect on you will have more impact. Use the list below as a guideline. I call this the *Circle of Influence*. Who is in your *Circle of Influence*?

Me

You are the most important person and at the very middle of this experience.

Family

Spouse, partner, children, step-children, grandchildren are usually close to the center, but not exclusively. They're closest to you by virtue of their presence in your home or by the contact they might have with you. Others may include parents, in-laws, sisters, brothers, nieces, nephews, grandparents, uncles, aunts and cousins. Depending on how close you are to each one, they will only enter into that "inner circle" at critical times. Know who these people are.

Medical

Doctors, nurses, social workers, chaplains, homecare workers, or psychologists are involved in your care in very specific and ongoing ways. You will have little choice as to their involvement, so it is better to take time to get to know and develop a relationship with each of them.

External

Beware of outside influences that are not represented in person but have great influence. This could be authors, books, the internet or famous people who have impacted you through their teachings and philosophies.

Friends

Best friends, acquaintances and past friendships will all want to spend time with you and are an important part of your life. They will take up some space that needs to be monitored.

Communities

Church groups, religious organizations, recreational teams, senior groups, hobby groups, etc., are communities you have invested time in. There will be certain individuals who will want to come and be with you.

Co-workers

People you work closely with and have spent many hours working alongside over the years are wondering how you are doing. They will make their way towards the inner circle to spend time with the person they miss.

Neighbors

If you have lived in a neighborhood for an extended period of time or have developed some intimate relationships, you will find people ringing the doorbell to see how you're doing.

Unforeseen

You may be blindsided by the unexpected. It might be an old friend you have not heard from in years or it could be a family member who returns after years of separation. It could also come in the form of someone who has "answers" to your dying. With a random phone call or visit, they show up on the doorstep with advice or a product that will cure you. Each can influence you and you need to be prepared.

Take a few moments to reflect on these individuals. How might they influence your story? The issue is not to eliminate them from being in contact with you, but to choose their proximity to you and how you will include then. If you do *not* want them "on your team," how will you best communicate that and create a boundary?

As mentioned earlier, some individuals will be in your *Circle of Influence* whether you choose them or not. So communicating with them in a manner that is kind and respectful is necessary for your peace of mind—you still have to look yourself in the mirror. Because these individuals may influence your story, you must be proactive and decide *how* you will be in relationship with them. Communication is your starting point here.

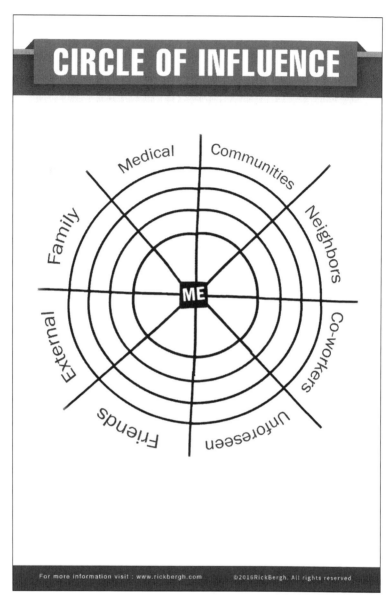

CIRCLE OF INFLUENCE

Medical · Communities · Neighbors · Family · ME · Co-workers · External · Friends · Unforeseen

Figure 1

CHAPTER 5

What Kind of Love Is Needed More Than Ever?

And now these three remain: faith hope and love. But the greatest of these is love.

– SAUL OF TARSUS

I could not understand why the nozzle did not fit in the opening of the gas tank. I was young. I had borrowed the car and it was low on fuel. I had pulled up to a service station to fill up the tank.

"What's wrong with this nozzle?" I wondered. "It's too large," I thought as I awkwardly began to fill the tank with diesel, despite the clumsy fit. Then it suddenly hit me. "Oh no! I just put some diesel in the gas tank of a car that only uses regular gas!!!" I quickly filled up the rest of the tank with regular gas. Thankfully it still ran, but there were some anxious moments as the car sputtered for a few moments on take-off. How embarrassing!

Wrong gas in the tank?

What keeps us moving in life is often the amount of love we receive from others around us. But are we receiving the right kind of love? If we're not, we might find ourselves sputtering along when we could be moving forward in overdrive.

Each of us has a love tank. In our relationships, if our love tank is empty or filled with the wrong gas, we won't be as responsive or effective.

Our greatest human need is to love and be loved, to know and be known. But what if we don't feel loved? How does that affect our relationships with people? Our happiness? If we don't feel loved, how does that play out when we're going through big challenges in life? When difficult or even traumatic circumstances interrupt life, the need to feel loved is crucial to our ongoing physical health, happiness and emotional stability.

The time following a terminal prognosis and the journey toward those final hours can be a roller coaster ride. Feelings of sadness, uncertainty, anger, loneliness, anxiety, loss of control—which may lead to forms of depression—need to be recognized and acknowledged as "players" in our final transition.

We will feel empty at times. This is fair. We are preparing to leave people we love. We may feel like the earth is crumbling beneath us. We need some stability. We need to feel some sense of security in the midst of our journey. Much of our security is based on the love that is extended to us from others.

Our emotional love tank can become very empty very quickly. We need to know we are loved and accepted. The assurance that someone is committed to our well-being is crucial. But even more important than knowing this in our head is experiencing it from another person who is close to us. Everyone needs to have loving care expressed to them in their own love language. If they don't, they shrivel on the inside. I will explain what I mean by "love language" in a moment.

I often see people soften during the final days of life. I have experienced family and friends expressing what I see as love in wonderful ways. But something even more powerful happens when each person involved in the "communal" dying experience feels loved back. This occurs when each one involved understands the significance of the other's "love language."

Dr. Gary Chapman's work on the *Five Love Languages* provides some of the most practical insights into putting the correct fuel into an empty "love" tank. Chapman theorizes that there are five unique ways people communicate and understand emotional love. These are based on our unique psychological makeup and the way our parents and other significant persons expressed love to us as children.[1]

Chapman's research on love language preferences has led me to apply it to my work in palliative care. Imagine the effect if everyone gave and received love in such a way as to fill each other's love tank consistently. We would have a different world. But what is my *own* love language and how can I know my neighbor's love language?

Everyone gives and receives love in a different way. It's just a matter of learning your own way of expressing love and then taking note of the other person's love language as well. It isn't rocket science, but it can revolutionize the way you care for others. If you are willing to learn another person's primary love language, you can become an effective conduit of love and be part of the filling-up process.

So what are the *Five Love Languages?*

1. Words of Affirmation

For some people, verbal compliments or words of affirmation are powerful communicators of love.

For the one with a terminal illness prognosis whose dominant love language is *Words of Affirmation*, what you say to them will mean everything. This person needs a cheerleader who can speak words of encouragement and hope into their lives no matter what they are experiencing. Here are some examples:

---

1 Gary Chapman, The Five Love Languages (Chicago, Illinois: Northfield Publishing, 1992, 1995, 2004).

- I'm so proud of you!
- You are an amazing inspiration to me.
- You are so positive, even though this is so difficult.
- I admire your tenacity.
- I am so impressed with your attitude in this midst of adversity!

You may believe that you are not helping out by being so positive in your words, but you are. You are *not* saying:

- I know you are going to beat this!
- You always seem to overcome adversity!
- I know you can do this and this will just be a blip in your life!
- Your positive attitude is just what you need to beat this cancer!

Those words are not reality for the one dying. People know when they are dying. They need authentic words that allow them to feel loved. When they do, they'll love you back. They want to know and feel loved by you so that they can continue to pour meaningful time into your life from an emotional love perspective.

How do you know if a person's love language preference is *Words of Affirmation*?

Consider the way this person expressed love all their life. What did they appreciate hearing in the past? This may help you to think about what they will need in the future. Did you notice a change in how your loved one treated or responded to you whenever you said one of the following?

- That was a fabulous meal you made!
- You're still working part-time and doing really well.
- Your home is spotless!
- You are really supportive of your kids' sports, aren't you?

If this person is affirmed, they feel emotionally connected to the other person, even if it's a brief comment or an encouraging smile.

If you recognize this love language in the person who is dying, you may want to review what's important in their life and affirm that aspect of who they were when they were able to be more active. Affirm those areas of life they were most proud of. What brought them joy and fulfillment? Affirm that. Yes, for certain, some of those important tasks may not be able to be duplicated now because of illness, but the words of affirmation still count. You can still find other words of affirmation that will help fill up their love tank.

2. Quality Time Spent

For other people, *Quality Time Spent* together is the key to filling up their love tank. This quality time must be focused and involve sympathetic conversation. If it's idle chit chat, then it won't serve the purpose.

Consider the stress, pressure, and emotions of the individual who has been told they must prepare for the end of their life. While words of affirmation may focus on what we are *saying*, quality time focuses on what the other is *hearing*—that you shifted your busy schedule to spend time with them, that you care about them, that you are interested in them and enjoy being together with them, even on this hard journey.

Quality Time Spent is all about understanding the thoughts, feelings and desires of the person you are spending time with. This listening must be genuine and uninterrupted, focusing upon the heart of the individual.

It does not necessarily matter what you are doing together—context is less important than content. It's that you are doing something with them and giving them your full and undivided attention.

Empathy is crucial for those with the *Quality Time Spent* love language. They need to hear: "I'm present. I'm here. I'm not going anywhere. I care about what you are going through. I don't have my cell phone on. I won't be taken away from you during our focused time together."

3. Gifts

Some people value receiving gifts as a symbol that someone cares for them. Dr. Chapman underlines the importance of symbols as having emotional value. We aren't talking about expensive gifts here, but rather simple gifts that make a person feel special and valued. It's not the size, nor the cost of the gift that's significant. It's a tangible item that can be held that says: "I'm thinking about you. You are important to me."

Dr. Chapman says that most people's love language can be easily identified because it's the way they express love as well. In this case, a person whose love language is *Gifts* will often be the giver of gifts. This person has been one of those individuals who has given gifts to many people and will continue to do that in order to express their love in a meaningful way — according to what they value most. *Gifts* is perhaps one of the easiest love languages to work with, because it's uncomplicated. It's never about the most expensive or the most luxurious gift. It's the thought that counts. It could be a simple card, one rose, a book, a letter, or a homemade craft. It does not matter.

For the one with a terminal illness and whose primary love language is *Gifts*, it's easy to quickly and effectively fill up their love tank. They will be waiting for you to bring them a gift and you will experience their joy as they open it up, no matter what it may be.

4. Acts of Service

Other people love to serve. This is the way they "love on" others and receive love. They will be scurrying around the home, doing chores, cooking meals, offering to fix the neighbor's fence, cleaning the house and making a meal to bring to an elderly shut-in.

Reciprocally, when an act of service is offered to them, they feel loved by the other person. So a person who is dying and whose love language is *Acts of Service* will truly appreciate what you do for them, the little things and the big things. They feel loved when you drive them to an appointment, bring over a meal, shovel their sidewalk, or vacuum their house. They are thinking about what needs to be done, so by helping them accomplish these tasks (big or small), you are filling their love tank.

One thing to remember about *Acts of Service* types is their own need to still be able to serve and not just be served. It's important not to take away everything from them, because serving is also their way of expressing love.

When Pam was in our home at the end of her life, we still found her tidying up, wanting to help cook a meal or fold her clothes. She liked serving as a way to express her care to her family. If we had totally taken that away from her, it would not have been helpful. She needed to feel she could contribute and *Acts of Service* was her unique love language preference.

Here are some questions to ask an *Acts of Service* person:

- What can I do to help you?
- Can you give me a list of the things that need to be done?
- What are some tasks that need to be completed today?

An *Acts of Service* love language has nothing to do with being bossy or demanding and everything to do with emotional connection and feeling loved. If a person asks for help with something, the help you give will fill their love tank. It's an emotional response for them.

5. Physical Touch

Have you ever noticed how some people prefer a hug instead of a compliment? They put their hand on your shoulder when they talk to you? These are the people for whom *Physical Touch* most affects their sense of being valued.

Of course, for a spouse, holding hands, kissing, embracing and sexual intimacy are all ways of communicating emotional love to one's partner. For individuals whose principle love language is *Physical Touch*, without it they feel unloved. With it their emotional tank is filled and they feel secure in the love of their spouse.

Other forms of touch are important and may not necessarily be expressed by a spouse but by a family member, friend or acquaintance. A warm hug, a handshake, a pat on the back, a cuddle on the couch—are all signs of warmth to the person who most prefers physical touch.

Knowing a person's love language will give you more "bang for your buck" as you love on the one who is dying. The one dying needs to be loved in a particular way, but so do the family members who are supporting and surrounding this person.

As mentioned previously, Pam's preferred love language was *Acts of Service*. I remember her staying up late at night to finish all of the home tasks: laundry, cleaning, kids' lunches, baking cookies for others, preparing for Brownies and her children's choir and early literacy program. She worked hard. She served us as a family and she served others as well.

I also know how much it meant to her when we helped out around the house, fulfilling our chore duties and systematically crossing things off that list on the fridge as we completed them. She liked to get things done, and if the kids and I didn't do something, she would. So I would get the car washed, the sidewalk shoveled and the vacuuming done before she got to it!

I had discovered early in our marriage that bringing roses home for our special anniversaries was not that important to Pam. Gift-giving was not the thing that turned her crank. She would say, "Thank you,

Rick, but we could use that money on something else." Daisies were her favorite flower, likely because they were the most economical.

Pam was also a very confident individual and although I would praise her for her gifts and affirm her as a mother, she would just smile and give credit to God. She would remind me that I needed to be careful how much I affirmed the kids. "Too much is not good," she would say. "They might become conceited or develop a big ego."

Pam was always busy, and I would have to haul her away to get her to spend time alone with me. We didn't have a lot of money, so we would go on a date to a restaurant and order a big cinnamon bun and share it. It was usually a short date because she would be wondering about the kids and thinking about the things she needed to get done. *Quality Time Spent* was not a big priority for her, but *Acts of Service* was. While Pam did like to cuddle (all of our family photos include us touching, holding hands or being close), *Physical Touch* would be her secondary love language.

It's interesting that even though *Acts of Service* was Pam's main love tank filler, it was difficult for her to give up a part of that control as people began to bring over meals, offer to clean the house, and fill in some of the natural acts of service during her initial treatments and recovery periods. But when she resigned herself, I felt that her emotional love tank was filled often and she was able to find the energy to focus on her family and friends as her body became progressively weaker.

If you would like to discover your love language, Gary Chapman's book entitled *The Five Love Languages* is an excellent tool. In the back of the book you will find a quiz that will help you discover the way you best give and receive love. This will in turn help you understand and express love in another person's preferred love language.

CHAPTER 6

Boundaries to Die By... Say What?

Don't ever take a fence down until you know why it was put up.

– ROBERT FROST

My family laughs at me when I park the car far away from other vehicles at the local mall or the fitness center. I want to protect my car from bangs, dents and paint chips. It works if everyone parks between the yellow lines. However, once one vehicle does not park properly between the lines, it affects the others next to them. It drives me crazy. It's a pet peeve of mine.

While I have included a lot of suggestions in this book, I want to tell you that one of the most important daily conversations you should include is around setting good boundaries. Examining these daily is really important because your situation changes daily and you need to choose to make your time on earth count—including who you want to be with you and how you will manage your changing circumstances.

When you have a terminal illness, you need to establish good boundaries.

Why is a boundary important?

Boundaries are an extremely important part of dying peacefully. The inclusion of boundaries needs to be considered and firmly set within the family unit, and with healthcare professionals, friends, co-workers and our extended community.

What comes into our lives needs to be examined for its worth and effectiveness. Learning to evaluate and establish boundaries is like a fence with a gate. You need to shut the gate when necessary and you need to open it when required. But you have control of the gate and who enters it.

Boundaries should be put in place to protect you and to help you die how you wish and with those people we want near you. Boundaries protect your heart and prevent unwanted words, people or experiences that impact you negatively.

Sometimes boundaries around the following are overlooked. Good boundaries are often established through our own initiative, by deciding to let others know exactly how we are feeling or thinking, what is not helpful and how they can be included in our journey in a positive manner. The choice is yours to make!

a) Curious questions

It's hard when people are talking behind your back wondering what's going on: "Did you hear? I heard that Robert has terminal cancer. I wonder how much time he has to live. How is he holding up? I wonder how his kids are responding. I wonder if he has everything in order."

Creating a boundary lets people know what's going on so there is no secondhand news, so gossip is not spreading like a virus. Erroneous information shared "across the backyard fence" about how you are managing will impact you more than you think. Be careful to share only what you really want others to know. Decide how you want this information to be shared and by whom. My motto is always *less is more*.

b) Details

Needing to know the details of everything that is going on is a selfish request. Why do people need to know all the gritty details of our lives? Is that what's important? If we choose to share those details, that's fine. However, we should never feel obligated. "I have cancer. It's terminal. I am spending the final days of this life as best I can with my family and friends." Is that not enough? Explaining the details of everything that is going on is exhausting. Don't do it unless you want to. Limit the conversation around your illness. Use the time for meaningful conversations. And let others know why this is more important to you.

c) Platitudes

Platitudes are really a sign of insecurity and of trying to come up with appeasing answers. People need to be very careful using platitudes. Often these are based on religion or scientific studies — and are used by people trying to lighten the intensity of the moment. But they can make the listener angry and frustrated. "Don't worry, I have a good feeling about this. God is going to heal you." or "Don't give up. Keep fighting." Terminal means you will die. Barring a miraculous intervention, you must be realistic and not allow other people's views and opinions to impede your final days. It's really okay to tell people that these kinds of comments are not helping you and you would prefer they not offer them to you. Be strong and be bold. Set a boundary by letting others know what is not helpful in their remarks. I needed to do this often for Pam. And I'm glad I did.

d) Interference

When you say you can relate or understand a person's situation because you have gone through something similar in the past, you are interfering with that person's story. "We went through this with my mom, so I know how you are feeling and what you are going through." No, you don't! Although a person may have empathy because of what they have gone through, you have learned in this book that everyone is different and each experience is unique. When people say that to you, kindly suggest that your story is unique and its outcome will be based on your uniqueness as a person. And remember your journey is not about them. You will want to remind them that you are the author of your own story and your story is important. Theirs is not important at this point. Unless you ask them their story, don't allow it to unfold into yours.

e) No

You need to learn when and how to say this word often and not be ashamed to say it. You also need to have family members say it for you in order to fend off the people who want to drop over unexpectedly, or call you on the phone. Often their intent is not wrong. People assume their actions and words are helpful, but they may not be at the particular time they have chosen. Be firm.

f) Medical questions

You have every right to ask questions and spend time with your medical team. You need to guide the conversation and ask whatever you feel is necessary. You also have the right to make suggestions to your doctor and ask for feedback. You also need to empower people to do this for you as you set up the parameters of this relationship during end-of-life care, when you may not be able to communicate as effectively as before. In my first book in this series, *Finding Anchors*, I devote an entire chapter to how to communicate with the medical system. You may find it helpful as you think about the relationship you have with your medical team at the end of life.

g) Lapsed family members

How close are you to your family? Some may return quickly and try to be heroes. You may find relatives or friends who want to come in at the last moment. Sometimes it's because of guilt. Sometimes it's a need to mend fences. For now, just be sure to be aware and to set the parameters of how this returning relative will be managed. Decide beforehand how he or she will be allowed to interact with you. Sorting this out may be difficult and some helpful advice is shared in Chapter 9.

h) Family members who won't let go

Family members vary so much in their feelings during this time and some will begin to interfere based on their understanding of dying, suffering and death. Their worldview or emotional level may influence or impact you and your family system. Although we must be sensitive to their views, it is more important to honor your wishes. Being clear on end-of-life desires and having someone communicate these effectively with all family members is crucial to a peaceful end-of-life passing. Again, I will focus on this process in Chapter 9.

i) People who want to visit

Whether it be in the hospital, at home or in a hospice setting, it is important for you to indicate your desire as to how often you wish to have visitors during your end-of-life journey. Visitors must not assume that their presence will always be helpful or necessary. Again, understanding personality preferences must be taken into consideration. A good boundary is you saying what you want on that particular day. People should never assume. Putting up a clear boundary and letting those who are caring for you know is important and necessary.

j) Near the point of death

There are some clear signs the body is dying and, although we can never predict precisely when death will occur, there are some important indicators. Asking the doctor or nursing staff these questions is legitimate and necessary. The final days are important. Setting a boundary with the medical profession around information shared at the end of life is crucial. It's fair to say, "I want you to let me know the progression of my disease. I want to know the signs that my time is getting closer."

Some family members don't want to know this information and are holding on to other possibilities. That's fair, but not always helpful. You need to let your family know that you are okay with death when it comes. And you need to be clear with each family member that you expect them to honor your wishes and not attempt to make last minute decisions based on what they might feel is the best decision for you. You have already made your decision clear.

k) Caring professionals who want to help

Your family knows you better than anybody and, although outside people can be helpful, your family should always take the initiative as primary caregivers. When there is confusion, questions or conflict that is difficult to understand, experts can be called on. There are people who are trained in this area, but their involvement should always be seen in the context of the family unit and what they can bring to the table that might be missing or helpful. Someone will need to set the parameters with all those who are part of the interdisciplinary team or extended caregivers for you. It's really your choice. Get involved.

l) Patient's wishes that are not honored

Clear directions should be given by you for end-of life-decisions. It is not fair for any family member or medical personnel to interfere with your wishes once you've decided. They should be legally written down, in your medical file, and a copy shared with the family unit. There should be no room for discussion once you have set a clear boundary that establishes your desires and wishes.

m) Friendships and tight communities

Family members will most likely be with you at the end of your life and during your journey. However, there are those outside your family who are important to you also. Your family members must know who these friends are and how you will want them to be involved at the end of your life.

n) Privacy around our failing body

As we get weaker and we become less cognitive, we wonder about privacy issues about our body. We may need more care. We may not be able to dress ourselves or we may struggle with our bowels. Who do you want present when these challenges come? This is an important boundary to put into place for your sense of personhood. Choose wisely.

There will be many people coming into your life during this final chapter. Each one comes to the situation differently. Don't ignore or push the needs of people away that need to be there and experience end of life in a meaningful way. But do put up boundaries so you can make the most of your last days and experience life to the fullest, even when it is coming close to an end on this earth.

Allowing people to care for you is important, but placing a boundary around your experience is even more necessary and crucial for a peaceful passing.

So from the beginning, let's park between the lines. Review the list above and park your life where and when you need to. You don't need a whole bunch of people running into you, leaving dents or chipping your paint when you are needing to say goodbye and rest easy in your final days.

CHAPTER 7

How to Manage Emotions That Keep On Rolling

Dying is a wild night and a new road.
— EMILY DICKINSON

Feelings are part of the human experience and are an integral part of who we are in relationship with one another. How we express our emotions will have a positive or negative impact on our relationships.

When I was younger, I owned a Honda Civic. I loved that car, mostly because it kept going and it was cheap to run. I was a student, so I had very little money, so when I filled it up with gas, it seemed like it would run forever. I had to budget my money very carefully, so I would often wait till the car was almost empty before I'd fill it up. That was okay in the summer, but in the winter it was not smart.

I discovered that all gasoline has some water in it and if you let the gas run out, the water would still be sitting at the bottom of your tank, potentially making its way into your gas line. You can guess what happened when temperatures hit 30 below. Yes, a frozen gas line. I ended up putting antifreeze in the gas line in order to thaw it out. But a couple of times that wasn't enough and I had to pour a small amount of gas into the carburetor to unthaw the problem down below. It was a lot of unnecessary work that I created for myself.

Sometimes we go too long before we address our emotions—and they freeze. We wait too long to deal with them and they get hard. Then there's the other extreme—an emotion that is expressed too quickly, in a reactionary way, may take us in a direction we didn't really want to go. So having some tools to examine what our emotion is saying would be beneficial.

Feelings have a function. They reveal that something is happening inside of you that needs to be considered.

You will experience a variety of emotions during the days that follow your terminal prognosis. And you will also notice those around you expressing their feelings in a variety of ways. Everyone who is close to you is trying to manage their internal reaction to this experience.

Some will choose not to deal with uncomfortable feelings and will attempt to push them to the background if possible. Others will express emotions without hesitation.

Emotions are the window into our heart. These deep emotions can sometimes come out as anger or tears, for example. When we see people responding like that, we assume we know what people are feeling. But that's not always true.

The outward expression of an emotion may not accurately convey what is truly going on inside.

It's always good to let an emotion sit for a time prior to responding, especially if it's an emotion that I call *hot*. A hot emotion is one you want to express immediately, without thinking its consequences through carefully.

Have you ever snapped at a person and then later recognized it wasn't the person you were actually mad or upset with, but it was something else going on in your life that came forward in an unexpected outburst? We have all done that before.

A family member had written a letter to us during Pam's cancer journey, and it said many things that were upsetting. The one that really got me was that our extended family was spending too much time on Pam and forgetting everyone else, especially his family. I was not happy. I did not lash out and engage him immediately. I called a family meeting, which included him, and we had a conversation. I knew it was deeper than what he had said, and it was. We all needed to let it sit for a time and then come together later.

We need to work hard at emotional management. The goal is to not allow a feeling to sit for too long and also to not allow it to be expressed too quickly, prior to examining it for its actual "story behind the story."

Each person will respond differently to the end-of-life experience of their loved one. Unexpected emotional outbursts are sometimes difficult for the one dying. But not knowing what others are feeling is just as hard. Looking behind the emotion that is dominant and examining the reasons can become an important daily exercise:

I might express anger, but the reason could be that I'm sad, not mad.

I might lash out at my doctor, not because I'm upset with her, but because my son did not show up to see me.

I might be quiet, not because I don't want to talk, but because somebody said something to me that upset me.

I might bark at my sister, not because she did anything wrong, but because I'm upset that my mom is dying.

Let's go back to my Honda Civic which seemed to last forever. I did not know everything about the car and did not realize that hidden in that little car was a small rubber (not metal!) timing chain in the engine block. It was not visible. Because I could not see it, I was not aware of its importance. Once this belt wears out, your engine blows without warning—which is what happened late one Friday night when I was on my way to see my girlfriend. Driving down a remote road to her home, my engine blew. What? I could not believe my bad luck. It blew on a rural road far from town — one that was not well-traveled. And it blew without warning.

Feelings are hidden until they are expressed. They can blow out of control if they go unrecognized or ignored. That's why *emotional intelligence* is so important. Recognizing the emotion, evaluating it and doing something with that feeling is a healthy and important response.

Unfortunately, many people are hesitant to express the emotion they are feeling, fearing they are making this experience about them. Remember, this is a communal experience and how you express what you are feeling will impact the one dying either in a positive or negative manner. Our words and actions are rarely neutral. They constantly advertise how we think without our even realizing it.

It's always better to share what you're feeling, if it's offered in a way that is honest, authentic and caring. So how do you do that?

The language we use to introduce the emotion is key to how the feeling can be expressed and received.

Blurting out an emotion or expressing a feeling without a *prelude* is not the most effective way of sharing it with another person either. Things are seldom resolved by that method. What do I mean by a *prelude?* It's a time of preparation in order to think through your words before you begin to share your heart. It is a start, but it is not the main event. For example, when I am upset, feeling angry or hurt — and I'm responding to a situation wisely — I will go for a walk and then come back and ask a question rather than make accusations. This has proven to be more effective (in my emotions being "heard") than has the "hit-and-run" approach when I blurt out reactively. Taking that prelude time has proven to be crucial.

While it may be tempting to want to verbalize our feelings indiscriminately, if you want it to be received by the other person, it makes sense to soften their heart by hearing them and discovering their heart first.

Let's return to the conversation we had as a family following the difficult letter we received. As the facilitator of this family meeting, I began by asking the person who was upset what he was feeling as we all met together. This pulled out the feelings that were expressed in the letter. "Could you tell us a little bit more about why you are feeling angry with us?" We allowed him to go first.

It's not a matter of agreeing or disagreeing with a person, but when you listen to the feelings and acknowledge them, you begin to go beyond the hurt to the heart. The letter writer had kept his feelings inside for a long time and they exploded in the letter during a time when a family member (Pam) was very sick. Can you see the perfect storm?

It was not an easy meeting, but I believe we were able to lay all the cards on the table and move forward in a civil manner. It would have been easy to put this off and say "not now." Not when Pam is near the end of her life. But we didn't. And I think it was an important part of her peaceful passing.

Always begin by trying to understand the other person first, before expressing your feelings. Check in with them and you will clear a pathway to their heart so they will be able to receive your feelings with openness.

In fact, it's important for the community to check in with each other as to what they're feeling on that particular day. You are going through one of the most difficult transitions in your life. Honest responses through a feelings-based evaluation will empower you to live authentically, because you are being truthful with yourself and with others. The feelings inside are strong and powerful indicators and protective mechanisms of what is happening and what you need to do next.

It's okay to stop in the middle of your day and evaluate what's going on inside. Often this evaluation will occur when something happens to throw you off your game. It stirs something inside of you and instead of allowing that feeling to immobilize you, sit back and consider why you're feeling it and what it's saying to you.

Don't be out of control with your feelings. Value their place in your life. As you go through the many approaches found in this book, emotions will rise and subside. You will be surprised at when and how they come, but don't be frightened by them. Honor them as something deep and meaningful within you and work with them.

Before you get going, spend a couple of days using the exercise below to reframe your emotions. Hold on to this tool as you begin to plough through the many emotions that could potentially blindside you.

1   Recognize and name the feeling that is most dominant in you right now.

2   Stop and let it simmer. Don't respond immediately. Sit in the emotion for a moment.

3   Evaluate it for its content. Examine the situation, background or context when the feeling first became apparent. Was there a reason the conversation took place? Who was speaking when your hot feeling emerged? Why did the conversation take place? Could you have misinterpreted its meaning? Sometimes the reasons for the feeling are fair and reasonable.

Ask yourself: Why am I upset? Is it because…

- it came from a specific person that I really don't like or trust?
- it came in response to something I said that was important to me?
- my thoughts or feelings were not acknowledged?
- somebody challenged my opinion and disagreed with me?
- the response came from a trusted friend who hurt me?
- a person slandered a value that was really important to me?

No feelings are wrong. What we want to be careful of is allowing the feelings to make us do something harmful to ourselves or to someone else.

Regardless of what this hot emotion is telling you, you need to take control of it. No one can change another person, only themselves. But you can choose *your* emotions.

4   Then choose a response that is smart and healthy. If it's a negative emotion that came about because of something someone said or did, decide if you need to talk to the person. Sometimes you don't. It may be something you need to examine in your own heart and resolve. Either way, reframe the experience, deal with the emotion, evaluate its ongoing impact and move forward for the greater good of the community.

CHAPTER 8

When Building a Team of Experts Includes Family

*The strength of the team
is each individual member.
The strength of each member
is the team.*

– PHIL JACKSON

I visited a man in a small rural hospital. He was dying. There was no palliative care program in the town and, because of this, the nursing staff would often ask me to come and visit people during their final days on earth. He was a bachelor. I did not know him but was happy and honored to spend time with this man at the end of his life.

He had no family nearby. He was pretty much alone, with only a few neighboring friends. We talked. His life was the farm — a farm he had worked hard to develop and cultivate from an early age.

The hospital was not his favorite place, but he knew he had no option since there was no hospice in the community. It wasn't long before I discovered that his farm was his pride and joy and took up most of our conversations. "I wish I could go there again," he said to me. "Let's do it!" I said. "Really?" he looked at me. "I don't think they will let me out of here," he said wistfully. "Let me talk to the doctor—I'll see what I can do," I said. I knew the doctor. It was a small town. The doctor did not want him to go at first. It was risky. It would be hard to transport him. "It's only 20 minutes away," I said to the doctor. "I will take responsibility," I added. So I signed the papers. We transported him to the passenger side of my minivan and off we went.

He was like a kid on his way to the circus that day. So excited. He gave me directions, pointing out all his favorite landmarks along the way. "There it is!" he said, lifting his frail hand and pointing. "That's my farm!" he said proudly.

We drove down the lane and he said, "Park over there, beside the barn." He could see his fields, the house, the barn and the corrals from that point. "I will leave you alone for a while," I said. "Just reach over and beep the horn when you are ready to go," I told him.

It was a good 45 minutes and then I heard the horn beep and I went back to see him. I could tell he had been crying. I just sat there. Then I said, "You have a very special home on this farm." "Yes, I do," he replied. And then he surprised me. "I wish I could die here," he said. I just nodded. "We can go now," he said.

I wish he could have died in his own home, too. I know it's not always possible to die at home and there are a number of reasons. For this bachelor, there were no family members available to be with him during his last chapter, and because there was no hospice in this community, he died in a hospital.

Most people prefer to die at home.

Pam wanted to die in the home we had bought and she had decorated so beautifully, in the home where she had created so many wonderful memories with her family and friends. We wanted to make sure we could fulfill her wish.

How could we make this possible for Pam?

What would be required in order for Pam to experience the very best care from us — her family — supplemented with healthcare professionals at home?

I know from our own experience, and that of others, that the decision to include palliative care in our end-of-life plans was a crucial component. We needed their expertise so Pam could receive the very best care possible. But it would mean working together. What would their contribution be and how could we best be involved as a family?

I felt from the beginning that we would need to work together as a team. We as a family would need to be perceived by the palliative care team as Pam's key caregivers.

You may not have knowledge about palliative care or understand its importance, so asking your doctor to provide information about this kind of care is important. Your doctor should be able to inform you about the best palliative care options when a life-limiting illness is diagnosed.

What do I mean by *life-limiting*?

The term *life-limiting illness* is used to describe an illness for which it is expected that death will be a direct outcome. We have treatments for many life-limiting illnesses, but a cure is not always possible. This could include, but is not limited to, chronic diseases, frailty (dementia) and cancer. The timeframe for each illness varies — but by requesting palliative care, it implies the imminence of death.

For Pam, we chose to have palliative care at home- by family and professionals four months prior to her death. Although we didn't know the timeframe (as is true with many illnesses), we knew that, because Pam was no longer able to accept any further medical interventions, her life on earth was limited. We also knew the history of the cancer she was fighting. Of course you always hope and pray (as we did) for a miraculous, last-minute healing. But that wasn't to be the case.

There is a psychological shift in choosing palliative care — a shift that needs to take place both in the one who is dying and in their family members.

I have heard people say that someone is "giving up" if they choose to no longer have treatments. There are usually some family members who feel that same way and who will push for more medical interventions. These may include experimental drugs, naturopathic means, new last-minute innovations in drugs or alternative interventions.

We did try some alternatives and traditional medicines for Pam. We considered the options carefully, but Pam said to me one day, "It's enough, Rick — we've done our best. We will leave the remaining days in the hands of God." Was that giving up? I don't think so. I wanted to honor Pam's decision.

Our plan moving forward did change. It had to. It was a tough thing to make that mental shift: we were no longer treating the disease with a cure in mind, but were giving comfort care to allow Pam to have quality of life as a priority in her final days.

When a family chooses palliative care, the following areas are of utmost importance: 1) Symptom Management, 2) Psychosocial Counseling and, 3) Spiritual Support.

Choosing a team of players who have the same goal and move in the same direction together is crucial to this kind of care. A palliative care team could include palliative care doctors, nurses, social workers, spiritual care providers, homecare professionals, volunteers and other allied healthcare professionals. Palliative care can be offered in hospitals, long-term care facilities, and in homes as well as in a hospice. Many people assume that palliative care is relegated to hospices only. But that's not true.

If you go the palliative care route, you will need to check for availability and ask about the specific program in your area. Only then can you decide how you as a family will need to be involved and what extra education you might require in order to feel comfortable in your role. You can examine which areas you would be willing to take leadership in during this important time in your loved one's life.

I believe the most important players in the palliative care team are you and your family. And families, wherever possible, need to take an active role within the palliative care team.

Here is the most important question you need to answer right now as you move forward in this journey: *Who is the expert in the life of the family member who is dying? Who knows them best?* I'm assuming you know the answer to this.

The second question is this: *Once you have checked into what the medical system can offer, what areas are you still afraid of that might prevent you or your family from stepping into this active role?*

What if you could honor your loved one's desire to die at home? What would you need so you could intentionally take part in providing what your loved one requires, thereby honoring his or her remaining days and allowing them to die in dignity?

The ongoing medical needs of your loved one are important. Why have we traditionally left this to the medical world? Can we as their family manage some of the medical needs of our loved one with some guidance and education? Are we frightened of this idea and should we be? What do we fear and how can we overcome these fears?

A. Symptom Management

1. How can I be certain that my loved one is not experiencing undue suffering?

It's difficult to see our loved ones suffer. We don't like to see anyone struggle physically, let alone someone who is precious to us. Some of the symptoms might include heavy and labored breathing, gurgling, bodily twitches, or unexpected verbal sounds like moaning. Sometimes it is more difficult for you to deal with the visual aspects of suffering than it is for the one who is dying. Often the one who is suffering feels bad for you — the caregiver — because they are seeing your reaction to them. Pam experienced physical suffering at various times, but she was also strong and vibrant in other areas of her life. I go into more detail about suffering and resilience in Chapter 14.

2) What will help me understand the natural progression of the disease as my loved one's body changes?

We can become anxious when we see changes in our loved one's physical body. Having some knowledge about the disease's trajectory and the changing medical needs as a result will be important. It's a conversation that can easily take place with the palliative care team. I was very pointed in my conversation with our team — seeking wisdom regarding the changes I saw taking place in Pam's body. I wanted to be aware of what I needed to do in response.

3) Will I be able to administer pain medication with confidence without professional assistance?

Pain management is tied closely to physical suffering. We want to be sure our loved is not experiencing unnecessary pain. Can we really manage the pain as well as a hospital, hospice or other facilities outside the home? Can we properly administer the pain medication and how will we know we are doing the best we can when our loved one cannot tell us as they near the end of life? These are legitimate questions to be sure.

We felt we were able to monitor Pam's pain level quite well, because we were with her all the time. We had clear instructions from our medical team and administered the pain medication at Pam's request. Because we were on top of it, we were able to mitigate her pain extremely effectively, right up to her last breath.

Again, a conversation with and information from your medical team will be important. That way you will be able to feel confident that you are making the best decisions based on the knowledge you have been given. You will also want to ask the medical team about the possible side effects of the medication. We asked all these questions on behalf of Pam and knew the answers to each of our concerns so our newly acquired knowledge kept us confident in the caregiving role.

4) What should I be aware of as death approaches? What should I expect at the moment of death?

If people have not been in the presence of someone as they've died, they might be frightened about the unknown. Conversely, many who have experienced the last breath of a dying person are surprised that it's not as creepy an event as they had expected. True, sometimes the body responds in ways that are not easy to see with our eyes as we watch it shut down. But we need to trust that the pain is being managed effectively.

Think about who you would want near you at the end of your life. What would it mean to you to have that person present as you took your final breath? What an honor it is to be there with someone as their spirit is escorted out of their body. What a peace it would give you to know that the very people you wanted to be with you at the end of life are there with you in your home at the time of your death.

We asked many of the above questions as Pam entered palliative care. We had open and honest conversations with our care team and supplemented their advice with ongoing instruction on how to best take care of Pam. These needs changed over time, but the more we asked to be involved with her care, the more the palliative care team talked to us. We began to trust each other.

Sometimes a medical care team is careful about giving out too much information because of the family's unwillingness to accept the reality of the situation. You can imagine how difficult this can be for professionals who are trying to prepare people for the death of their loved one and yet are being met with denial or even rage.

We were willing to listen and accept their expertise and wisdom. Our questions were pointed. We asked for clear answers to our questions as we prepared to say goodbye and experience Pam's final breath on earth.

Here is a list of questions you might want to ask your medical team:

- What are the signs that the body is shutting down?
- What should we look for?
- If this (event) happens, what should we do?
- How can we be sure that (name) is not experiencing pain?
- What can we expect near the end of life?
- What are the possible side effects of certain pain medications?

While we have just confronted some of the fears regarding the alleviation of physical symptoms and suffering, there are also other important aspects of dying that people are frightened of that need to be addressed here. We are, after all, heart, mind, body and soul and we have many relationships that need to be considered in the whole picture.

B. Psychosocial Considerations

Many receive quality end-of-life care by trained professionals if they have chosen palliative care early enough in their journey. But most people don't choose that initially and much is missed that is necessary for a peaceful passing. As people come to terms with their imminent death, there is often a massive scramble to "get ready" for what is now facing the family members, both individually and as a family unit.

One of the most difficult aspects of dying is managing everyone else's role, their participation and the roller coaster of emotions from family members and friends.

The decision to engage in the last chapter of one's life seems counterproductive for some. That's because some people don't see life in dying. Or, if a person has previously experienced a bad death event, they prefer to stay at arm's length. Still others really want to help and do whatever they can, regardless of their own fears. Further along the continuum are those who over-engage and become controlling, which has a negative effect on the rest of the family. Unwittingly, they impact the person's peaceful dying because of emotional and relationship disruption or bullying.

Each one of us in our family had to find our place in this journey with Pam.

All of the children returned home to be with Pam during the last three months of her life. It was an important part of their lives, sometimes very difficult, but many beautiful and important moments were shared between the children and their mom.

I was fortunate to have 25 years of professional experience when we went through this. I had learned from hundreds of end-of-life experiences what components were required for a peaceful passing. I knew what might be missing based on past experience and tried to be proactive in our family's situation.

The psychosocial elements of dying are often the most challenging. Families tend to neglect these important things, leaving them to happenstance.

What do I mean by *psychosocial elements*?

How people respond and react emotionally, cognitively, existentially, spiritually and relationally to this unique experience will be different from everyone else.

What we feel, think, believe and how we relate to one another may begin to unravel if we believe that our unique perspective is the *only* perspective. That's why it's important to think about strategies that let others know how we will operate together as a family.

1. What should I do with my emotions and those of people around me?

The emotional swings of family members and the one dying can be quite varied. Gaining knowledge about emotional management is crucial in helping each person discern what is going on in their own life as they transition along the dying path to the end of life. Our emotions impact those around us, whether they are expressed or not. We rub up against each other. Deep thoughts, apprehension and questions can result in sadness, anger and a myriad of other emotional responses.

We should not leave emotions untapped. Emotions are the gateway to our feelings and feelings tell us what is really going on deep inside us that needs to be noticed, explored and recognized.

Does every family do this well? Not at all. But they could.

I watched as one woman kept walking out of the hospital room where her father lay dying. In the hospital room she sat at a distance in the corner. The other family members moved in closer toward their father. She only looked on. She would come and go every ten minutes or so. I noticed this pattern and after a while I decided to follow her out as she walked down the hallway. "May I join you for a walk?" I asked her as she went out for a smoke. She nodded her head. I said nothing. She took out her cigarette, lit it, had a puff and threw it to the ground and started to cry. She threw her arms around me. "What's going on inside?" I asked her. "I just want to sit by my Dad and hold his hand," she replied through tears. "I feel angry and sad at the same time," she continued.

We talked for a while longer then returned to the hospital room. I sat by her Dad and held his hand. A few moments later I said to her, "Come on over and take over for me." She came and sat down next to her Dad. She looked into her dad's eyes and whispered, "I love you, Dad." He whispered back the same words and she held his hands tightly for a long time. What was fascinating was the reaction of her mother and brothers who, deep down, knew this had needed to happen for some time, but did not know when or how it would take place. Each of them had a few tears. Tears of release.

Be open and honest about what you are experiencing internally. Lay it on the table. It is always best to share your emotions, despite any trepidation you might have. Whether it's the person dying or a family member who is being affected by the death, communication is key. Relationships can get choked really quickly when either people aren't honest about their emotions or emotions get expressed inappropriately and harmful words are spoken.

If you return to Chapter 7, which deals with emotions, you can use it as a template to aid in having conversations about your feelings. Each person communicates his or her emotions differently. Being sensitive to personality differences (and more specifically to the way in which we take in information, process it and share it in our unique timeframe) is helpful. These are called *preferences*. After you do the work of emotional intelligence (which means examining the emotion you are feeling and learning to reframe it), you may find it helpful to go to the specific family member or even the dying person and have a conversation with them to clear your own heart. But reframe first so that a hot emotion doesn't cause hurt instead of healing.

Here is a simple strategy that works:

- I'd like to share with you a feeling that I've been experiencing. It's...
- I have taken a closer look at how I'm feeling and I think it's hard for me because...

If the feeling you have has the potential to *separate* use this statement:

- I wanted to share this feeling with you because I don't want it to...

If it is a feeling that has the potential to bring you *closer* use this statement:

- I wanted to share this feeling with you because...

No feelings are wrong. However, you want to be careful that HOT emotions (like anger, frustration or jealousy) do not make you do something harmful to yourself or to someone else. Be proactive by identifying and sharing often what is going on internally. It is good medicine for us and good for every person we are in relationship with on this journey.

2. How can we best invite others to share what's going on inside of them while still focusing on our loved one?

It's challenging to keep the family pulling in the same direction as death nears. At times you will see trouble starting to brew. That's because everyone is experiencing the death differently. Some people are thinkers and some are feelers; some are living with regret and some are at peace. Each person will process death uniquely.

Who manages the relationships that come in and out of a dying person's life? Sometimes these relationships change over time and sometimes they come in externally and blindside you. In Chapter 6 I spoke about the importance of boundaries that need to be honored so people don't feel overwhelmed.

We should carefully consider the influence of people coming in and out of the person's environment where he or she is dying. One toxic relationship can make a peaceful passing impossible.

I have developed a simple strategy called "checking in" that can help keep potential problems at bay. Checking in can either involve the person who is dying or those who are part of the "circle of influence" (the community being affected by the death). "Checking in" is like a psychosocial barometer that works in a community setting.

Checking in with the person dying (first priority):

- I'm wondering how you are doing with all the people wanting to be with you?
- Are there some that you find challenging to be with?

- Are there people you would like to see more of in the next few days?

Checking in with family members (second priority):

- Are there any family members that you feel are bringing something toxic to this experience?
- Are there any 'elephants in the room' that you feel we need to discuss as a family?
- Are there any members of the family that seem distant, quiet or overly aggressive?

Checking in with the palliative care team (third priority):

- Have you seen any family members that cause you concern?
- Have you noticed any emotional reactions that trouble you?
- Have you observed any discontentment in our family?

Checking in with trusted friends, pastors or confidantes (fourth priority):

- How well do you think our family is working together?
- Is there anything you think we should be discussing with the palliative care team or family?
- Do you think someone should be brought in to facilitate conflict resolution issues?

As I've mentioned in earlier chapters, there is usually one person in the family who is more gifted at bringing people together in conversation. If you don't have someone who is an agent of reconciliation in your family, find someone who is qualified to facilitate the conversations.

People who are dying know if there is trouble in the family. It's not fair for the dying person if family members do nothing to resolve these issues when there is conflict. His or her time on earth is limited and resolution allows them a peaceful passing.

George had been given a terminal prognosis. We had spent many hours together prior to this and had been engaged in many end-of-life conversations. He was good with God and had come to the realization that his disease was limiting his days on earth. I went to visit George and his wife one day. As we sat having a cup of coffee, I asked him the simple questions: "What are you most worried about today? What's at the forefront of your mind?"

After some thought, he answered, "I'm not worried about myself. I know where I am going when I die. But I'm worried about my son, Rob. I would like to talk with him and spend time with the rest of the family." Most of his family lived on the other side of Canada. "Let's get everybody together," I said.

Two weeks later, we gathered in his living room again with all of the children, grandchildren and their spouses, including his estranged son, Rob. It was the beginning of significant family conversations. All that needed to happen was for them to be educated on important matters that should take place at the end of life. Facilitating the discussion simply gave them permission to continue to work as a family unit. They just needed to recognize, from their dad's perspective, what he required in order to die peacefully. I emphasized how important this would become for the whole family as well.

3. What can we say or do when our loved one feels they are being a burden?

Many people who are dying begin to feel they are being a burden on their loved ones and the sense of guilt overwhelms them. They see us tired, giving up our activities, taking leave from our jobs, or spending time away from our families in order to be a caregiver.

There are two important steps family members can take to assure their loved one that it is a privilege and honor to be with them in this chapter of their life, no matter how long it will take, because time with them is truly a gift. First, you need to take care of yourself in order to rejuvenate. Second, you need to affirm to your loved one who is dying that they have purpose and meaning in your life.

We need to be honest. Caring for the dying is exhausting with the many tasks and the emotional swings that accompany the end-of-life journey. We must recognize how much energy and time it will take to have a loved one die at home. You will need to be vigilant about taking care of yourself. Some of us may not have the emotional and physical energy reserves to do our best and may need a break. You will need to recharge.

Compassion fatigue happens in family members who have decided to provide 24-hour care at home for their loved one. You need respite from the situation as primary caregivers. Yes, you have decided that this is important and worth giving your time to. But, you will get tired and need to be recharged — it is just part of having good boundaries. When your loved one sees you taking time for yourself, it gives them peace of mind that you will be okay. Exercise, nutrition, rest, nature, time to reflect — all these are important for your ongoing survival.

Pam used to say to me, "Go and have a beer with your buddies, Rick. I will be fine." She somehow knew that it was important for me to rest or to get away in order to come back to her rejuvenated. Sometimes I did not want to go because I wanted to spend as much time as I could with her, knowing her days were numbered. But I realized how important it was for me to remain healthy in order to serve her the best I could. Having a beer with my buddies was part of my relaxation program!

Having other family members around is also really helpful and can alleviate some of the pressure. So is a homecare team. It's about a shared communal experience with all who can be involved, based on their time constraints.

Ask your loved one who they might want to share some time with them during the final chapter. This can become a shared communal experience. What are some of the other communities available to lend a helping hand along the way as you take a needed break?

We were fortunate not only to have family members wanting to be with Pam, but many from our community of faith offered to be with Pam when we needed some time to rejuvenate.

The second strategy is to affirm your loved one in their purpose and role in *your* life. If they are feeling like they are being a burden, then they need to be reminded of how much they mean to you.

I will speak of this more extensively in Chapter 9, but for now you may want to talk to your loved one as much as you can in the present tense. Living in the present is important and while your loved one is thinking about your future without them, they need to have your full attention in the "now." Engage them in life now. Share your life. Ask for their opinions. Get their feedback. Seek their wisdom. Tell them what's new. Let them know the latest in your life and invite them into your world. They will need to see that they are contributing to your life in a positive manner. The rhetorical question they need to be able to ask is, "How could I be a burden when someone still wants me and needs me?"

4. How should we understand and manage unexpected grief responses?

Family members will begin to experience feelings of loss before their loved one dies. Anticipatory grief begins prior to death when we begin to miss what we know we will no longer enjoy after our loved one has died. This is often expressed emotionally or behaviorally.

As we think about our loved one, we begin to reflect on what we are going to miss and we are sad. As we come to the realization of this fact, we may tend to also want to move forward knowing that this person will no longer be a part of lives on earth and so we might as well look forward to what's next.

This is difficult because we then feel that we are not always present. We move ahead too soon. This is a natural part of life that pulls us forward. It feels like a catch-22.

Being honest with what you will miss is an important conversation you may want to have with your loved one—it could result in some amazing heartfelt conversations.

Here are some conversation starters that you may find helpful:

- These are things I'm really going to miss about you...
- These are the times in my life when I am really going to miss you...
- These are the important events in my life that I will hopefully have in the future that I wish you could be with me...

C. Spiritual Questions

Dying can be a very spiritual experience and if the person does not recognize it, they may become anxious if it goes unaddressed. Even if the person has not been active in a religious organization previously, he or she will most likely be asking questions about God and the afterlife.

Also, many people have death awareness experiences that must be honored and listened to carefully. Simply pushing them aside as "hallucinations due to pain medication" or "the result of drugs being introduced into the body" is not helpful. If someone asks questions related to spirituality, where do they turn?

If there is no one in the family who feels comfortable with that, no chaplain, no church community, where do you go?

The old adage says, "The two things you should never discuss are politics and religion." But what if people want to talk about them? I have visited many dying people and one of the most important questions I ask is very simple: "Are you scared of anything?" The response that I have heard over and over again from people is, "I'm wondering if this it or if there is a 'next'?" or "What happens to me when I die?"

This begs a deeper exploration of spirituality that should be examined and discussed out loud with people who want to.

Who does the work of spirituality? Perhaps there are chaplains who are available. Or maybe not. If you are dying in a home, do you have this available to you? If you belong to a religious community, then you are fortunate. If not, you need to think carefully about who can and will facilitate this work.

Do not ignore the spiritual exploration of the dying or the existential questions that beg a deeper conversation. It may not be an important part of *your* life, but it may become something significant for your loved one. Besides, their exploration into the soul might stir up something inside of you. And there may be a teaching moment waiting to happen in some deep place in your life as well.

Good questions could include the following:

1. What is your perspective on God as you look back on your life?
2. Do you think that God is interested in you and your current circumstances?
3. What would you like to say to God if you had the opportunity?
4. Have your ever thought about life after death and what happens after you die?

In a family I got to know, the wife was a faith believer. Her husband was what she would have called "marginal" in his belief of God. But as he lay dying in the hospice, questions about what might be next began to preoccupy his thoughts. She phoned me and asked if I could visit, which I considered an honor. You stand on sacred ground when you are invited into this experience.

He had questions about God. I never begin with my own understanding of God. I always just ask simple questions (like the ones above) and allow people to come to their own understanding prior to sharing my views. If they want to know more about where I stand and what I believe, they usually ask.

He had been in this place for a couple of weeks and had not yet been asked any spiritual or existential questions. He could not wait to discuss these important matters with me. It was a beautiful time of exploration, which ended with me sharing the message of forgiveness, grace and hope as found in the message of the Christian faith. The message grabbed him and he handed over his death and dying to Jesus.

It reminded me so much of the story of the thief on the cross in the Bible. Here was a man who was being crucified along with another criminal and Jesus. Both the thief and the criminal who had been convicted of murder were paying the consequences for their actions under Roman Law at that time. The one criminal looked at Jesus, who had done no wrong and yet was experiencing the same punishment as he was. It captivated him. Somehow he had already heard about this Jesus guy before because he said, "Jesus, remember me when you come into your kingdom." Jesus' response is simple: "Today you will be with me in paradise." No fuss, no muss, no church, no baptism — just forgiveness.

People who are dying are on a spiritual trajectory. We need to recognize and explore this with those we love, honoring their search as holy, mysterious and significant.

My wife, Erica, recently made a discovery that was important for her as a choral conductor. It was at a concert in Montréal, Québec, Canada. A choral conductor generally leads a choir through a piece of music, creating an ebb and flow of nuance with his or her gestures. It is then the singers' job to interpret the gestures and respond accordingly as a group.

But one day she discovered a new phenomenon and shared it with the audience. She said, "Sometimes a conductor may need to get out of the way and let the singers just sing, own the music and create something new as they breathe together." She gave them their notes and sat down in the front row. By the end of the piece, tears were running down the cheeks of those teenage singers. A standing ovation erupted. "I got out of the way," Erica said, "and let them sing. They looked and depended on each other and not me. But it was hard for me to give up control and sit back and just listen."

My role as a pastor was always to begin the facilitation process and encourage conversations to occur naturally over time. I have learned to get out of the way and allow families to talk. Now I just want to encourage people to come together and enter into a story. I'm not the author. I'm the gatherer. I no longer interfere, but invite people to ask a few questions that might be helpful.

I soon learned also that the final moments of life on earth were ones that should be shared mostly with family, not necessarily with professionals. Once in a while people would ask me to stay with a dying person. My response to them is often: "I am not going to take this moment away from your family. This is your time." I usually learn later that conversations took place that would not have had I been there. What does this say about the importance of asking questions and leaving when necessary?

When Pam requested to die at home, I was not frightened. I was a little nervous about the journey, but I was not afraid of how we could manage or provide for her in the days that followed.

True, I had experienced similar circumstances because of my profession, but soon realized it was not so much that I had all of this extensive training that allowed us to be comfortable, but rather a commitment as a family to do our very best to honor Pam's wishes.

By facing the concerns and questions we had about her dying at home, we were able to get the necessary help we needed and support each other and Pam right until she took her last breath.

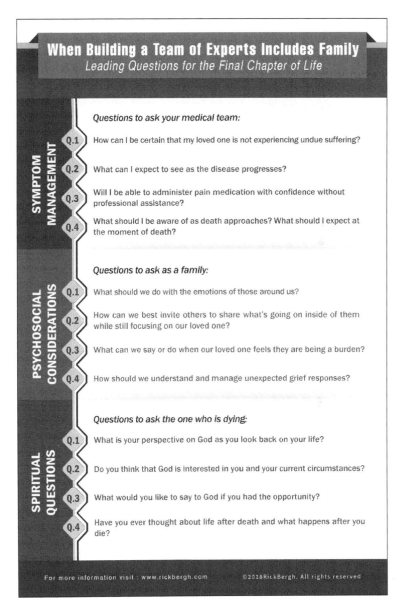

Figure 2

CHAPTER 9
Directives, Wills and Funerals — Front-End Loading Particulars

Failing to plan is planning to fail.

– ALAN LAKEIN

F ront-end loading is important. What you do *now* will make it much easier for your family in the future.

Wouldn't it give you peace of mind to enter your final chapter of life knowing you have done everything in your power to help your family make wise decisions on your behalf? The best thing you can do for yourself and for your family is to clearly lay out your end-of-life plans and details while you still have all your mental faculties.

Having important and robust conversations *now* will take the guesswork out of your final days and help your family transition through loss effectively.

Most dying people want to have conversations about the end of life, but aren't sure how to broach the tough topic with their loved ones. Being intentional in your conversations and putting things into place will give you peace of mind.

When we hear the words, "It's important to get your affairs in order," we wince. These words represent the sad reality that life on this earth is coming to a close for you or a loved one. Unfortunately, many people, perhaps afraid to admit the inevitable, are not proactive in getting many important details settled. Clarity while you are still living is key to peace for you and for your family.

You may think and believe your family would never have disagreements about end-of-life decisions—but you might be surprised. I have experienced many "normal" families who have become estranged very quickly when final wishes were not followed or expressed clearly.

To be honest, Pam and I had a basic Will but that was about all. When Pam was diagnosed with cancer at age 42, a detailed Will and a Personal Directive were not really on our radar, let alone an Enduring Power of Attorney. Besides, I didn't want to talk about these details with her—I felt this would make me appear negative, focusing on the question, "What if?" and sounding hopeless rather than hopeful. And I wanted her to live so badly.

In hindsight, I wish we had discussed these important matters together earlier, when she was still healthy and when we weren't thinking about her cancer journey, her dying or her death. I know better now and have learned from my experience. Because I was not particularly wealthy, I concluded estate planning was something only rich people did. I know better now.

As we entered into the final few months of Pam's life, the conversation around her last wishes became very important. Pam and I talked about her funeral and she made suggestions about the songs she wanted played or sung. She wanted me to preach (because she said I was the best preacher she had ever heard). We talked about the promises we made to help our kids out with their first homes—a promise I continue to honor in her absence. We put in place her Personal Directive, which included her final medical wishes.

Were those conversations easy? No! But they were very important.

Here is a checklist of topics to think about and discuss with your family in order to avoid confusion or, worse, family divisions.

1. Legal Will

Question: I have worked hard all my life. I will have some assets left over. Who do I want to leave the fruits of my labour to?

Legal Wills cover the distribution of the accumulated assets in your estate. You will need to choose an executor (a trusted family member, friend or professional, such as a trust company) who will oversee the distribution of your assets once you are deceased. This executor is obliged to communicate your last wishes with all those named in the Will, so consider carefully that person's communication and relational skills.

Just a note regarding *Planned Giving* (*Legacy Giving*) — your Will can become a teaching tool for your family. You may want to consider giving some of your resources to a charitable organization that has made an impact on your life or the lives of others. Most of these organizations have experts who will help discuss the specifics.

Consider the impact of where and to whom you will distribute your personal assets. It is good to reflect on this because of the potential problems it might leave following your death.

2. Enduring Power of Attorney

Question: I'm not sure how I will die. It could be sudden or as a result of a terminal illness. When I am no longer able to make personal financial decisions for myself because of my mental capacity, who do I want to fill this role?

An Enduring Power of Attorney is given to a trusted family member, a friend of sound mind or a professional, such as a trust company, to make *financial* decisions on your behalf.

When you lose the capacity to make your own decisions, it must be confirmed through an assessment. You usually name someone in your Enduring Power of Attorney to be the one to determine whether you can make these decisions or not — often this is a family doctor who makes that call along with a family member in accordance with applicable provincial or state legislation.

If you don't name someone to assess you or the one you chose is not available, two medical practitioners may make that decision on your behalf. Please check with your lawyer as to the legal requirement on assessment guidelines.

Think about all of the financial decisions you are currently making. Write them all down. If you were no longer able to make these decisions, what directives would you like to leave to someone and who do you trust to make these decisions on your behalf?

3. Personal Directive

Question: I am no longer able to make decisions on personal matters because of my mental capacity, who will make these decisions for me?

A Personal Directive is a very significant document because it deals with two important aspects of your life:

1 Everyday personal matters that impact your ongoing living with dignity when you can no longer make decisions, and
2 End-of-life decisions with regards to your dying physical body (primarily medical treatments you would or would not want).

Sometimes this document is temporary (for example, if you regain your mental ability to make decisions). On the other hand, if you had a serious brain injury or a progressive condition (like Alzheimer's Disease), you would require this document for the remainder of your life. Having this in place will allow you to have control—as much as is possible—if you are no longer able to make decisions about your life because of limited mental capacities.

A Personal Directive applies while you are still living and covers personal matters and medical matters (specifically end-of-life decisions). This is a legal document and must be followed. But it deals only with *personal* matters and end-of-life wishes, not finances (as does the Enduring Power of Attorney).

A Personal Directive allows you to name someone (an agent or agents) to make personal decisions on your behalf, as outlined by you in your Directive.

Such areas might include:

- your healthcare
- your accommodations
- with whom you live and associate
- your participation in social, educational and employment activities
- legal matters that do not relate to your estate
- your temporary care
- the education of your dependents who are under 18 years of age

The second part of a Personal Directive should take into consideration the following questions:

1   *I have a terminal illness prognosis and am no longer able to make coherent decisions because of my mental state. What would my final wishes be?*

2   *What if I had heart failure or a stroke and was unconscious? Would I want to be resuscitated or not?*

3   *If I was in a vegetative state, what would my final wishes be with regards to medical treatments or interventions?*

4   *Where would I choose to die and spend my final days if I had a choice?*

5   *What will be my decision with regards to organ donation or the use of my body for medical research?*

The two important issues that you must bring clarity to are whether you want to prolong your life through heroic measures and whether you want to withhold treatment (including artificial life-sustaining treatments or procedures) at the end of life.

These may include, but are not limited to:

- a DNR (Do Not Resuscitate)
- a feeding tube when you can't swallow
- a life-support system
- an IV for hydration
- a transplant
- a blood transfusion

Other decisions that should be made are:

- pain medication administered to relieve pain, even if it hastens the moment of death
- decisions regarding organ donation
- the choice to enter palliative care at a certain point in your illness
- a personal choice to enter a hospice as death approaches

Because medical advances occur every day, it is better to remain flexible in the naming of specific medications, treatments or medical equipment so as not to eliminate newer and improved options. This is why it is also important to review this document on an ongoing basis as new information comes your way, both personal and medical.

Because this document honors your wishes, your agent(s) should reflect your values and belief system. You can go to www.rickbergh. com/lookingahead/familydiscussion to download the document that will get family conversations going. The document also includes questions to ask with regards to capacity assessment—which is a crucial part in determining when and how a directive begins and ends.

4) Supported Decision-Making Authorization

Questions: English is not my mother tongue and I don't understand what the doctor is saying to me about my condition or my medication. I need someone to convey back to me what the doctor is telling me. Where do I go for that?

A *Supported Decision-Making Authorization* (also called a *Substitute Decision Maker*) allows for someone to attend doctor appointments with you; share information about your health records when you are weary, don't understand the language or need an extra set of ears; ask questions on the phone that need answering; help when you are deaf and need someone to communicate; or communicate your decisions to the medical team when necessary.

In this scenario you are completely lucid and capable of making your own decisions but need a supported decision maker for legitimate reasons.

As you age and deal with complicated medical language that can seem foreign to you, it is important to have someone who is able to guide you through the barrage of information coming at you.

Taking steps to implement the legal stuff:

1   Speak with your family members about the above four areas, inviting them into the conversation. Consider their input. Teach them the value of putting into place these documents and the reason why they are important.

2   Take the information you gathered to your doctors, spiritual advisors or any other important people in your life. Get their input. Ask for clarification. Once you have this information, go to a trusted lawyer. Ask the lawyer for his or her professional input and get this paperwork completed. Get a Will, Personal Directive and Power of Attorney done and in your hands.

3   Call a family meeting and share the final documents openly with those who are important to you and give copies to them. Be sure your own copies can be easily found and accessed, whether at home or in a safe deposit box. Give copies of your Directive to all your physicians and to those who are caring for you as well. In some cases, it can also be registered with a government body.

It may surprise you how many people do *not* have the above documents in place. I know from my counseling and pastoral experience the fallout from not having a Will in place is really messy, both financially and emotionally. I have also experienced the horror story of families fighting over last wishes when their loved one is dying because the information was not written down. I often ask those diagnosed with a terminal illness if they have a Will and Personal Directive in place. They balk at first until I explain the consequences for their family, friends and organizations they support.

I have frequently had workshops in my local church to talk about end-of-life considerations and their importance and was always amazed at how many individuals put off this important task. You need to do it now — it's not age dependent and needs to be reviewed on a regular basis as life shifts or transitions happen.

If you are really proactive, hire someone to help you with estate planning and get going on this now if you are healthy. At the very least, put the above documents into place without delay.

You need to know that money is a potential separator for your family. I have seen families that had been close become fierce and act awful toward each other. You will need to be transparent with your closest family members.

All four of my children have a copy of my Will, Personal Directive and Power of Attorney. They know precisely what my wishes are and who I've named as executor. They also know what will happen financially at the end of my life as a result of this discussion. They know exactly what I want if it comes to the point where my body is shutting down or my brain ceases to function.

The clearer you are with your family by sharing your plans, the better and more peaceful your family will be.

You do not need last-minute heroes or estranged family members to swoop in at the eleventh hour and make all the decisions. Make them yourself when you are strong, not when you are physically weak or mentally struggling to make important decisions.

I have been involved with families where clear end-of-life wishes (especially medical intervention) have not been discussed or written down in a legal document. The healthcare system and doctors are often forced to make life-changing decisions to keep people alive when they know the chances are slim for a full recovery. This becomes a nightmare for families and medical staff and potentially divisive for families down the road.

One woman's daughter came in from out of town. She had not spent much time with her mother during her terminal illness. But now she was home. The other daughter was the mom's caregiver and knew her mom's desires and wishes quite well—that her mom did not want to be put on life support in the case of an emergency. Her mother had spoken of her intentions to her one "caregiving" daughter, but had not written them down. The estranged daughter came in and took over. It was awful, long and nasty. The sisters still do not speak to this day. There was nothing in place to allow the verbal decision of the mom to have any merit.

This is very important: just because you have been appointed an attorney or an agent in a valid legal document does not give you the authority to fulfill the wishes of that person unless they are written down, legally certified and presented to the medical team as a legal document. Don't mistake one for the other. That is why having a paper trail is so important. It doesn't just save money; it saves relationships.

Much unnecessary pain may happen because of not having this information readily available when differing family members are pressing in emotionally with their own agendas.

We all want a peaceful passing. We all desire for our loved ones to be with us at our death. No one needs to live with animosity due to misunderstanding or misrepresentation when they're breathing their last. Having the conversation around these matters leads to deeper relationships with family members and can bring you closer together, so that you are working from the same page.

Another important family discussion and decisions you should make are plans for your funeral, memorial or celebration of life service. Directions regarding your funeral can be included in your will (not in your personal directive, which ceases to have authority once you are deceased) so as to make this process as easy as possible for your family members.

A funeral service is for those left behind—not for the deceased—as odd as that sounds. Though you are no longer physically present, that does not mean you should not think of those who are remaining and trying to live life without you. A service of some kind helps people celebrate your life and thank God for who you were in their life. It brings people together for support and encouragement. It speaks words of hope for the future and yet acknowledges the pain of missing someone important...you.

A memorial service is the first step in healthy mourning. It helps people move forward even in the midst of their grief. Here are some things your family will need to know about your funeral service:

- Where will the service take place?
- Who will preside at the service?
- Who do you want to deliver your eulogy/time of memories?
- Who would you like to choose as pallbearers or honorary pallbearers?

- Will you be cremated or have a full burial funeral?
- What music would you like to be played?
- What family or friends would you like to be involved in the service?
- Should there be a reception or lunch to follow? What would you like to have happen at that reception?
- What special additions would you want to have at your celebration of life? Do you have a video to be shown or a letter that needs to be read?
- Where will you be buried?
- What do you want on your headstone?
- What funeral home will take care of your arrangements?

While dealing with these front-end loading particulars is not easy, it's smart. People who are dying want their family to continue to be a family that loves each other, even amid the most difficult decisions. Being proactive in these things can help alleviate family tension later on.

Please note that this is not legal advice. Check with your lawyer to receive professional advice that will protect you. Be sure to refer to your local government's legislation with regards to end-of-life matters.

CHAPTER 10

How to Continue the Story When You Get Stuck

We don't have to be afraid of dying because it's not really death that scares us. We are afraid of not having lived.

– HAROLD S. KUSHNER

I love listening to people's stories. I know from experience that questions help people move their own narrative along. Questions help people see the value of their life's story.

Recently I was watching a movie that was being streamed live. I was on the edge of my seat as the mystery unfolded. It was near the end of the movie and the plot was getting very exciting. It was a real nail-biter. And then all of a sudden… the screen froze. "You've got to be kidding," I yelled out loud. "This is crazy! I need to know what is going to happen!"

I tried to get it going again. I turned the box off and on. Nothing. I unplugged the power source and tried to reboot. Nothing. I turned the TV off and on. I checked everything twice and finally after 15 minutes of frustration, I gave up, bewildered and annoyed. I wanted to know the outcome of the story. I wanted to know how it would finish. How would it turn out for the main character? I never did find out. It made me a bit angry, especially since I had watched it right up to the very end.

When I spend time with people who are dying, I know their narrative is not finished yet. So I engage them in a way that continues their story. There are more experiences, more encounters and more living to happen right to the end. It is streaming live, right in front of you. We don't want the story to freeze as it nears the end.

I've discovered there are questions that help the dying with their "writer's block"—questions that help continue their story, expand the narrative, move it forward, or even change its direction when it wants to finish early. You may think this is inappropriate when someone is nearing the end of life, but these moments are often the most poignant and powerful moments of a person's story.

In the past 30 years, I've been with hundreds of people as they died and I have learned something from each one of them. But I have also noticed some patterns in the dying—five areas that keep coming back—areas in which the dying seem to need some coaxing of one kind or another. These are the areas I press in to by asking questions.

Why do I feel this is important? Why do I bother? I bother because people often wait too long to pen their final chapter. If steps need to be taken, things need to be said, wrongs need to be righted, it's too late once you're dead. The final chapter isn't just for the dying, it's for those who live on after you're gone.

A prolonged death can be both a blessing and a curse: a curse, because no one wants to see you suffer, but a blessing because of the opportunity it affords to say the things you need to say and make final and lasting connections with loved ones.

I have heard many times, "At least my mom is at peace now." When I hear those words, I think to myself, "I actually think you are the one at peace now." Would you not want inner peace prior to death? Would you not cherish these words coming from your loved one: "I am at peace. What about you?" It goes beyond their acceptance of their own death to include the satisfaction they have as they look back on their life, reflect on significant relationships and prepare to move on to what might be next for them.

Although I have spent many hours with people in a palliative care setting, which allowed them time to reflect and talk, I have also been called in at the later stages of people's illness in order to be with them in their final few days and hours. I'd like to share with you the things I've learned from hundreds of people. These are the five areas that come up over and over. I'm not advocating dying as a linear approach but as an opportunity to be intentional for the greater good of the entire community.

1. Three Powerful Words

She phoned me late one night. I did not know her but she was a Lutheran and had found my name, Rev. Rick Bergh, in the phone book. "The doctor told me my husband does not have too long to live and I should let the family know. My children do not know how serious it is and I have not told them," she continued, crying softly on the other end of the phone line. "Could you please tell my children for me?" she asked.

She had three children, two boys and one girl. They were a ranching family. "I told my kids that the pastor would be here tomorrow morning and I was hoping you could meet them at the main entrance of the hospital before they come in to see their dad. He's really going down hill," she said.

"Of course I can be there," I continued. I was a rookie pastor and had no clue how to effectively communicate this difficult news to these three children. I had never been asked to do this before. But I was determined to do this well—it was my first church to take care of.

Some families have trouble sharing bad news with each other. This mom was one of them. I visited her husband in his hospital room.

He said very little and seemed to hold his emotions close to himself saying, "I'm a man of few words. I know my family loves me. We don't talk too much," he stated bluntly.

The children began to arrive at different times. The daughter managed to slip by but not the two boys. The first son came in through the hospital entrance — the best description I can give is that he was a true Budweiser man: jean jacket, boot cut Levi's jeans, black worn out cowboy boots, and a dirt-caked cowboy hat. His moustache and whisker stubble did a poor job of hiding the wad of tobacco in his mouth. He was one tough-looking dude, as was his brother who came in later.

I introduced myself to him and said, "We should have a chat before you see your dad. Your mom asked me to meet with you." We went into a side room and sat down. I did not hesitate to share the difficult information. Deep down, I'm sure he knew what was happening. "Your dad is dying," I said. "The doctor said he doesn't have much longer. That's why your mother asked you to come today," I fixed my eyes on him without flinching.

A nod of the head was all the communication I got from him — and later from his brother. And they both looked down at the floor as I talked and shed no tears. We sat in silence for a few moments. Then I continued, "I'm not sure," I said, "but if my dad were dying, I'd want to share three words with him." He looked up at me from under the brim of his cowboy hat. "These might be the three most important words your father would want to hear from you before he dies," I added. I did not know if what I was saying was helpful or not, but I said it anyway and watched the story unfold — from a distance.

He went in to see his Dad. I waited outside in the hallway to give them space. This happened both times with each son. Each one in turn came out of their dad's hospital room, tears streaming down their faces. Later on I learned from their mom that those powerful words "I love you" were expressed that day to their father for the first time ever and those same words spoken back from father to sons.

I went back into that hospital room as the family gathered around the bedside to see a father and husband. They were talking, sharing, and holding his hand. I saw a father smiling. I saw a family united.

We all understand the power of words. I have seen their effects in people's relationships as a counselor and pastor. You have seen their impact on you. They can build up or destroy. We sometimes use words loosely. We don't always think about the significance of our last words spoken.

When people tell me their mom or dad never said "I love you" to them, it saddens me. You can excuse it and chalk it up to culture, upbringing or resign yourself to "well, that's just the way they are," but it does not mean it's okay. Those three words are important for people to hear, whether they admit it or not. If you are nearing the end of your life and have never said those words to your loved ones, perhaps it's time.

It was 29 years later, last summer, when I met up with the mom in this story. I went back to celebrate the anniversary of the little church I had pastored. This woman came up to me and I did not recognize her—not until she reminded me of that night and the impact it had on her sons. She said, "Thank you so much. My boys still speak of you when we think back to that night when you supported us as a family." I did not do much that night, and I really did not have to. I just got out of the way and gently invited them to consider three small words of great significance.

Are there people in your life to whom you would like to say, "I love you"?

2. The Forgiveness Factor

A few years ago, a woman phoned me whose husband was in the hospital. He was dying and he was scared. "Could you please visit him?" she asked. I was a pastor and was often called on to do palliative work in this small community.

As I got to his room, I greeted him and asked casually, "Hey, Peter, what's up?" He said, "I've done some really bad things in my life, pastor." I paused for a few seconds, looked at him and said, "Oh… you too, eh?" He smiled. "What's going on?" I asked.

"I did something terrible over 20 years ago. I stole a man's wife away from him in this community," he confessed. Then he began to cry. I sat there in silence, honoring the moment. Something from deep inside this dying man had just been shared with me. I felt privileged that he would entrust me with this story and wanted to respond appropriately.

"What do you want to do about it?" I asked. "I want to tell him that I'm sorry," he answered. "Then do it," I responded. I'm always very intentional and proactive in my approach. "But I'm scared to phone him. Would you call him for me?" he asked. "Sure. Give me his name." I wasn't at all surprised that I knew John — it was a small community. So I phoned John that night.

His initial response wasn't exactly positive. Fair enough. Given the nature of the request, he was ambivalent about going. However, when I spoke to him about his *own* heart and what perhaps needed to be freed as a result of this offense, he agreed to go. I wasn't sure what would happen and I chose not to be there at the meeting — even though they had both wanted me to come. This was about their relationship and what each man was carrying in his heart as a result of this painful experience.

Two days later I went to visit Peter again. He was very weak. He was even having trouble talking. His death was imminent. I was curious to find out how the conversation had gone — or if it had gone at all. Perhaps the conversation never even took place? I shuttered at the possibility that maybe forgiveness hadn't been extended, or that John never went in to visit Peter — it happens. What then?

"So, what happened?" I asked Peter. "Did John come to see you?" "Yes," he replied, nodding his head and smiling. "Well?" I continued. "He forgave me. I told him I was so sorry. He told me that he was not perfect either. Then we shook hands. Thank you for calling him," he said. "You are welcome," I answered. Peter was tired and dying. He closed his eyes. His wife sat next to him. She took me by the arm and whispered, "They say he does not have much time." I held her hand as we looked at this man whom she loved dearly and would miss deeply.

That was last time I saw Peter. He died the next day. I was honored to preside at his funeral. I could not help but think about the power of forgiveness in a man's life. Not only did it change Peter but it had a profound impact on John's life as well. How do I know? Because I spoke with John later and he thanked me, telling me he had been holding on to hatred for Peter for many years. But those few minutes in Peter's hospital room had changed him forever.

None of us is perfect to be sure. That makes the act of giving or receiving forgiveness all the more powerful.

When given a terminal prognosis, the most difficult aspect of dying is the notion of leaving close family members behind. Relationships are usually at the forefront of the minds and hearts of the dying — loved ones who are close but also (and maybe even especially) those who are at a distance or estranged.

People want to leave this earth without feelings of guilt or regret surrounding their relationships — the fact is, many of us are not close to family or friends. Sometimes this is because of distance and sometimes because of bad choices made in the past.

Is there anybody you would like to see that you have not seen for a while? There may be a good reason to see them again.

3. Paying It Forward

Generativity is an important term that was coined by psychologist and psychosocial theorist, Erik Erikson. It focuses on investing in those who will outlive us, leaving a legacy to the next generation, contributing to the lives of others and seeking to be remembered for our good. Almost always it's about how we will impact our families or friends, whether we have children or not.

One family I ministered to was not talking. At least it seemed like their conversations were not very significant. The dad was dying and I had a few good conversations with him. Of course there were the usual regrets, things he wished he had done differently, but his story was important and, deep down, he wanted to know he had made a difference. He was a very successful businessman, but he had come to the conclusion that all his hard work wasn't nearly as important as he had thought. Now he wanted to be an influence in the lives of his children and grandchildren.

His family was not overly communicative—their way of coping was to use humor or chitchat. Nobody wanted to talk about Dad's dying. In fact, they were frightened by the prospect of his death. Most of them stood in the corner of the hospital room, far away from his bed. His wife sat beside her husband, holding his hand. He was silent as everyone talked around him.

His wife was concerned about the children and grandchildren. They were not talking to their father. Everyone was ignoring what was going on—it was clear to me that their dad had something to say, but there was no room for him to say anything. "Can you help us?" she asked as she followed me out into the hallway. "I can meet with you as a family tonight if that works," I replied.

As I arrived back in the hospital room that evening, there were about 12 family members gathered. They seemed to be waiting for something to happen—they wanted this facilitation. They wanted someone to take some leadership. They had never done this before, so how could they be expected to know where to start?

I launched in, "So your dad's dying and you don't know how long he has left. I think it's important to do some things together, but tonight we are just going to do one thing. If you are not comfortable, it's okay—the choice is yours. I want each of you to tell your dad (or grandpa) what he has taught you in your life that is most important to you. You need to share a story or a memory to go along with it if possible. We will each take a turn."

There was an air of nervousness in the room. But after the first one shared their story, the others followed suit. Everyone shared that evening. It was a beautiful experience of laughter, tears, joking and seriousness. Not only did each person share what dad / grandpa had taught them, but he, in return, spoke back into their lives about how each one was special to him and what he loved most about each one uniquely. After his funeral, the family thanked me for having encouraged them to share that night. Some of the same stories made it into the eulogy.

Have you taken time to thank your loved one for their impact and influence in your life?

4. Legacy Building: "Tell Me I'm a Good Man"

One of my favorite movies is *Saving Private Ryan*. There are many challenging scenes in it—scenes that reveal the consequences of one's life choices. But one of the most powerful lines of the film comes at the very end when Private Ryan, now an older man, stands looking at the grave of the captain who died while rescuing him. Recalling the Captain's final words to him at Normandy—"Earn this!"—Ryan turns to his wife and says, "Tell me I've led a good life. Tell me I'm a good man."

Most people, whether they admit it or not, want to know they have lived a meaningful life. We call this *legacy building*.

- What was my life all about?
- What was my purpose?
- How did I do?

Legacy building means much more than simply a list of your accomplishments. It is less about achievement than it is about life lessons and wisdom that can be passed on. You may want to write these things down in order to preserve them. Consider it your very own *time capsule*.

How will you be remembered?

How do you *want* to be remembered?

If you buried this "capsule" and it was found 100 years from now, what would people say about who you were and about the life you lived? This should be an honest reflection of all your life, the good, the bad and the difficult. What nuggets of wisdom have you gleaned from the way you led your life?

This is not your eulogy—it's your life's story being honored. Here are some areas you might want to consider as you review your life.

a) Family Heritage

Everyone wants to know about family history—it's the bedrock of identity, whether you are adopted or blood-related. I don't know how many times I have heard people say, "I wish Mom (Dad, Grandma, Grandpa) had told me more about their life. There is an amazing connection that happens from generation to generation when we understand how our parents and ancestors lived.

A good question to ask is: "Tell me about your childhood? What were you like as a teenager? What do you know about your family heritage that you would like to pass on to me?"

b) Life Accomplishments

It's a positive thing to look back and articulate all those events in your life that were significant.

A good question to ask is: "Could you please tell me about what you are most proud of looking back at your life?"

c) Life Values

Your values develop mainly from your family of origin but also from life's experiences that shaped you. What worldview was foundational for you? What events molded you?

A good question to ask is: "Could you please tell me about your most important values that have helped you in your life?"

d) Life Struggles

All of life is filled with ups and downs—but it really is the hard times we go through that teach us the most. So often we like to share the mountains but we are not ready to talk about the valleys and how they changed us.

A good question to ask is: "Could you please tell me about the most difficult times you faced in life and what you learned from them? What mistakes instructed you most?"

Legacy work is really important. It sets you up for a lasting and impactful influence in the lives of your loved ones in the future.

5. What Is My Purpose Now?

My grandpa called me into his room. He was dying of cancer. He was very weak. He said, "Sit here with me." He took hold of my hands. "Ricky," he said to me, "stand firm in your faith. You are going to be an excellent pastor." And then he asked me to pray for him. I don't know how many times in my life when I became discouraged in ministry, I heard my grandfather's words coming back to help me press in.

My grandfather could not do much, lying in his bed sick. But his purpose found its way in my life that evening, a few weeks before his death.

A big part of dying is the ongoing commitment to live purposefully—this probably sounds like an oxymoron. Purpose is linked to what gives us meaning. It's also linked to personhood, which asks two important questions: "Who am I?" and "How do people see me?"

Just because you are dying does NOT mean you no longer have purpose, but that your purpose looks different now.

A wonderful opportunity exists for a dying person to build into the future of their family and friends by affirming who they are and sharing the vision they have for each one in the future.

These words can be significant for the ones living and impact them for the rest of their lives. Positive and affirming words can be replayed in the minds of loved ones and inspire them. The converse is true as well—negative words also carry impact, but not the kind that brings life. Recalling words of vision and affirmation reminds us of the deceased and reinforces their influence in our lives. I often remember the words of my dad, my grandpa, my grandma or Pam. I recall these words and they give me hope and joy as I continue to live my life forward.

We should be reminding them in what ways this is happening to us and thank them. We should be recognizing what they are doing in other people's lives and remind them of their ongoing contribution. This sense of who they still are for us affirms their importance in this chapter of life.

When I visit the dying, I often start my conversations with these statements:

- *I'm looking forward to learning from you today.*
- *I'm hoping you can share some wisdom that might help me in my life.*

Then I might ask the following open-ended questions.

- *What have you been thinking about lately?*
- *Have you had a conversation with a family member recently that was important to you?*

When I am caring for family members, I will often say, "When you are with your loved one who is dying, listen carefully to their words, observe their actions, tap into their experience. They are coming from a deep place where you have never been. From deep places come treasures they may want to share with you."

A good question to ask is: "How do you feel you can best contribute to other people in your life right now?"

The last few months of Pam's life, I wanted to sit on the edge of her bed and learn from her every day. She was like a never-ending well of living water feeding my soul and life.

I'm really glad I was able to tell her that I was sorry, that I loved her, that I was proud of her, that I had learned from her, and that I would always miss her.

She is still having an impact on us today and we carry her well-lived life in our family's fabric.

I guess that means she is still making a difference in our lives.

Well done, Pam!

CHAPTER 11

How to Guarantee a Return on Your Investment When You Are No Longer There

*Even if I knew that tomorrow
the world would go to pieces,
I would still plant my apple tree.*

– MARTIN LUTHER

M y grandfather was a mechanic. He taught me some important lessons about vehicles that I now apply to other areas of my life. "Take care of the small things now, because it will prevent bigger problems in the future," he would always say. And he was right! It seemed to me that my vehicle would usually break down when I was furthest from home and even further from my mechanic. Ever happened to you?

When I was young, I didn't worry too much about breaking down on the road. But once I had four children and a wife and was traveling in –30 degrees Celsius down the highway, I began to prepare for possible unexpected outcomes and eliminate as many potential problems as possible. So although I could not predict the bigger problems, if I took care of the smaller things, bigger challenges were less likely to occur.

Just by checking my tire pressure, oil, fluid levels, battery connection, windshield washer and blades, and hose connections, I knew I could eliminate some of the possible challenges. Not being trained as a mechanic, I made sure I checked those things more often, especially when we would go on extended road trips. I couldn't control the unexpected, but I could take care of those things that were within my control—like vehicle maintenance.

Interestingly, we prepare for almost everything else in life—except our death and dying. Somehow we tend to let it unfold as we saunter down the road toward our final destination.

What we do in the final months, weeks or days of our life is worthy of reflection. Look ahead and see what steps you can take to alleviate at least some of the grief of your loved ones who are left behind. We know there will be grief to be sure, but are there things you can do to lighten their grief by being intentional prior to your death?

There is a story in the Bible about Jesus. He knew he was going to die. He gathered his disciples together on the night prior to his death. What did he do? He shared the Passover meal with them and brought new meaning to it by his words and actions.

We have come to know this as the Last Supper. The most important words Jesus spoke to the disciples were, "Remember me every time you eat this bread and drink this wine." This has come to mean something much deeper for believers in the Christian tradition. But for the sake of this discussion, the creating of this poignant event by Jesus himself, as one of the last rituals, was amazingly important to connect his followers to himself forever in a very specific and intentional way following his death.

I want to share with you a few stories that showed how Pam was thinking about us even though she knew she would not be able to share in the family's ongoing story after she died. She cared deeply about our future and our happiness. She thought ahead for us.

High school graduation was a significant ritual and rite of passage for our family. We did it up really well. We would rent a special facility. We would have the meal catered. Tons of family would be invited. I would write a silly song that the kids would be forced to sing about the graduate. It was an amazing experience for each of our children.

I think the most special part of the evening were speeches delivered by many of those who were present. Grandpas and grandmas, siblings and, of course, mom and dad. Each of our children except Landon had graduated and gone through this experience. Landon, our youngest, would be going into grade 12 following the summer of his mom's death. Pam knew she would not be present for Landon's graduation, but a month before she died, she handed me an envelope with Landon's name on it. "Read this to Landon on his graduation day," she said. I cried.

On the afternoon of Landon's graduation, we gathered in our home, each of us giving our speech to affirm Landon. I said, "I have one more speech to give, but it's in letter form. Landon, it's from Mom," I continued. It was an amazing connection to a mother who was not able to be present on the day of his graduation, but was there in essence because she planned ahead and considered the needs of someone she loved. There were many tears that day.

Although Pam spent many hours talking to each of her children, she also prepared a letter in her last few weeks of life, with help from her sister Carol Ann, to be given to each of us at a later time. To this day those letters are special to our children and to me. Each child pulls their letter out and reconnects with the words of their mom in a very intimate way at different times in their life. Pam was thinking about what we might need that would be helpful in our journey.

Lovell was a good friend of Pam's who had some treatments for breast cancer and seemed to have pulled through. We were thankful. Lovell was also an amazing sewer and quilt maker.

I didn't know at first, but as Pam realized her life was not going to last much longer, she got together with Lovell and began to design a special quilt. A couple of months before she died, she told me it was to go over her casket—and I wept.

She designed it with Lovell and on the top it said, "Home with Jesus." It hangs on our den wall with pictures of our four children on either side. Why would she do this? Why was it important? She wanted us to look at this quilt and be reminded of the most important message—she was thinking about us.

Pam loved Christmas. She loved to do it well—it was always a special time for our family. She had Christmas decorations down pat, each having its proper place in our home. I really did not pay too much attention. I only knew that everything looked beautiful and festive.

The thought of decorating the house for Christmas without Pam there was burdensome to me—it was Pam's gifting, but clearly not mine! My girls were off at university and were about to come home for the holidays, so I forced myself to bring the Christmas decoration boxes in from the garage and begin the onerous process. I opened the boxes and wondered where on earth I should put all this stuff. Then I saw it... attached to each decoration was a label and a diagram outlining where it needed to go in the house. On the garland, in Pam's clear printing, were little tags attached to each piece, showing me which railings they belonged on throughout the house. I stopped... and began to weep. She knew how hard this would be for me and she lightened my grief by thinking about me in her last days.

I wonder sometimes if part of our purpose in dying is to think about how we can help others to live joyfully without us, even though they will miss us.

What are some things you can do that might lighten the grief load for those who remain after your last breath? What can you do ahead of time?

CHAPTER 12

Why You Begin to Move On Before You Want To

Dying is something we human beings do continuously, not just at the end of our physical lives on this earth.

– ELISABETH KUBLER-ROSS

When a person is dying, there are a myriad of losses that occur all at the same time. These become challenging to manage, as each loss is significant in and of itself. These losses impact the ones who are close to the one who is dying as well. So you've got compound and multiple losses happening at many levels for many people.

I remember watching Landon kiss his mom as he went off to play hockey one evening. It was too difficult for Pam to go to the arena. In the past, our children had fond memories of their mom cheering them on from the stands in all of their sports. Pam couldn't do this now. Two losses were occurring. Landon missing his mom's attendance at his present events and thinking about her not being there in his future and Pam missing being there now and in the future as well.

You need to consider the role of these and similar losses occurring during this final chapter on earth. These are known as *concurrent losses.* These are losses that are happening as byproducts of dying. You are already beginning to say *goodbye* to many things along the way.

Any illness is about loss. It requires that you ask deeper questions about what you think about yourself. Am I still me? Who am I now? What is my purpose? Do I still have purpose? In the dying process, everyone questions his or her personhood. It's a raw and real time. It can't be otherwise.

You used to be good at certain things and were gifted in those areas. But now you are experiencing the loss of no longer being able to do what used to come easily. As tough as it sounds, it's time to reframe. You still have much to give and much to receive.

We usually talk about *reinventing ourselves* when we change careers or transition into new and challenging circumstances. Oddly enough, these final chapters of life on earth also require an inner resilience that is similar to reinventing oneself. Here is some self-talk you might want to consider:

> *"I continue to be myself in the midst of the many changes and losses that are occurring in my life as I journey this path with my family and friends. But I feel different. And I need to be honest about that as well. And I need you, who are most important to me, to let me know how you are feeling and perceiving this experience as you think about letting go of all that has been part of who we are together."*

Loss is not always a bad thing. Why? Because loss drives us into a deeper exploration of what it means to let go. And these series of intentional *letting go's* prepare us and others for the time we will no longer be physically present in our friends' and loved ones' lives. To enter these conversations is healthy and proactive.

Everyone else around you is likely experiencing loss at some level, too. That's not easy. Even if it's not expressed verbally, each person is in a pendulum swing of emotions and uncertainty. Fears permeate people's thoughts:

- I will be a widow
- I will be a child without a mother
- I will be a sister without my sister
- I will be a mother without a child
- I will no longer have a spouse
- I will no longer have living parents
- I will no longer have a best friend
- I will no longer have a grandparent

You will need to be aware that each one is going to miss you in some very unique ways, and they are thinking about that very deeply as they see you become weaker.

As humans, we anticipate loss and mourn what we will no longer be able to have in the future, even if we're not there yet. We know it's coming. This generates grief prior to the actual death and triggers something called *anticipatory grief.*

My last year of college was like this. I had such an amazing experience that year that during the last two months of class I found myself feeling intense loss at the thought of being done soon. I still remember the last day. As the resident head, I would have to be the last one to leave, making sure all the rooms were cleaned and all was in order. I had to say goodbye over and over again to all 47 people who were in that dorm. By the end, I was the only one left. Then I had to say goodbye to who I was in that particular context. I felt as though I was being forced to say goodbye to myself.

Why was it so difficult?

I did not know at the time that I was experiencing *anticipatory grief,* but that's what it was. I was unconsciously processing every-thing I was going to miss about my college experience. I wanted to do more of what I would miss before it was taken away from me. So I played more ball hockey. I visited more friends, often late into the night. I knocked on more doors for a visit. I found myself going back to places where memories had been made: hockey rinks, bars, and parks. I was trying to recapture all those significant events and people that I would miss so much.

It was a powerful experience. And even though I knew I would have an amazing future, I was still living out those intense emotions of detachment.

Grief is what happens on the inside. It is our human response to missing what we no longer have that used to be significant to us. *Mourning* is our public expression of grief as we attempt to move forward, discovering what will be different while still missing something very special in our life.

This happens also during the last chapter of life. We begin to experience and think about all those things that we miss, some of which we can no longer participate in because of our new and ongoing limitations. We notice those "missing parts" and so do those around us. We are letting go, even though we may not want to and our sense of who we are begins to change as a result of this reality.

Asking who we are now and coming to grips with that is key: "What can I do to help myself as I reflect on what I am going to miss? What can I do to help you process your grief while I'm still living?"

I would think about my life without Pam. I did not want to, but I did. I knew her life on earth with me was limited because of her illness. My mind was preparing me for the inevitable. I would just begin to experience some sense of resolve or peace—and then the next day the grief would come rushing back at me like a tidal wave, making me incapable of acknowledging my eventual loss. I went back and forth.

I would think about my children and their lives without their mom. I couldn't bear the thought of them not having her present in their lives in the future. It was sometimes overwhelming for me and I would spend hours crying when I would go for walks by myself.

Anticipatory grief carries with it a tremendous sense of guilt: you are thinking about the person's death while they are still alive. You begin to accept the reality of their death, but in doing so you start to move on in your emotions. But you can't! They're still alive! Then you feel horrible for having those thoughts. It's not that you wish them to be dead, but you are living with a foot in both worlds. This is completely normal and is the dichotomy of *anticipatory grief.*

Pam woke me up one night. "I need to talk to you," she said. "Okay," I replied. She looked at me and grabbed my hands. "Rick," she continued, "when I die, you need to get remarried." "Pam," I replied, "I don't want to think about this right now. We are not giving up. God can still heal you," I blurted. "Rick, it's okay. I know you. You cannot survive without a good woman in your life," she said with a smile. "And do it sooner rather than later." I cried as I held her close.

I was already grieving the death of my wife whom I would miss so much. And at times, I wondered if I'd ever find a "good woman" again. I was anticipating what was going to happen and moving on, at least in my mind, in small ways. It's hard to live in both of these worlds — the world of the present and the world of the future.

It's important to recognize what is going on inside and to recognize how it might impact our individual relationship with the person dying.

If we find ourselves unusually irritable one day or responding irrationally, it may be because we are anticipating what we will miss and are living it internally before it happens.

Grief begins before you want it to and the work of mourning starts to happen before it should.

Pam had not died yet. I wanted to make it to our 25th Anniversary, but Pam just got weaker and weaker. We missed our 25th anniversary by 9 days. I had a good marriage but I missed out on our 25-year mark.

As Pam got weaker, I thought about not being able to share that special day with her and realized I was already grieving before she died.

This will happen to you as well as you sit beside your loved one and ponder the future without them—and it's normal.

The guilt that comes with *anticipatory grief* is very hard and emotionally exhausting for everyone involved in this story. It's not because we don't love or care that we are starting to move forward. Life pulls us forward—it isn't stagnant. Life is never motionless. But you feel like you are being pulled in two directions: straddling what is now and what will be.

Find a good friend to speak with about your feelings—it's a tough conversation to have with a family member. I have heard people say, "He's already thinking about the future and she's not dead yet!" So discussing your very real feelings with a friend can avoid the misunderstanding or perception that you are cold-hearted if you were to have that same conversation with family.

Be kind to yourself. I loved Pam and wanted every moment to count, but I also needed to identify what I was going to miss and my response to it. It's a good thing to take notice and understand how others around you might be struggling with similar feelings, what each of you are going to miss and how that might come into play in your ongoing novel as you continue to pen its outcome.

CHAPTER 13
Removing the Obstacles for a Peaceful Passing

If you can get yourself where you are not afraid of dying, then you can move forward a lot faster.

– TED TURNER

The factors that contribute to a person's anxiety over death are not always easy to measure.

Not knowing when death will actually occur, what the journey toward it will be like and the questions around what happens at the moment of death leave people feeling anxious or disturbed.

What are some factors that might contribute to higher levels of anxiety?

For 30 years as a pastor, I sat with people who were dying — often late at night and into the wee hours of the morning. As I observed these deaths, I gained a unique perspective that has shaped my ongoing work with those who are dying and sometimes afraid.

The question really becomes "What are you afraid of?" And when that is answered, figure out if it is possible to lighten the load by taking away some of the components that are adding to your present state of anxiety.

If peace and anxiety are at opposite ends of a continuum, wouldn't we want to always be moving toward peace? "How can I become less restless? How can I manage what is happening in my life, when I haven't experienced this before?" Some find this transition so difficult that medication is required for their anxiety.

We need to consider what is being added to our life that may be contributing to more anxiety than necessary. We know we will experience some stress. That is normal. What contributes to your anxiety? Can it be removed? What contributes to your peace? Can more be added?

In my professional work, I began to notice when and how anxiety levels started to change in the people I had the privilege of being present with in their final days. In addition, I saw the effects certain factors had on the person that—once recognized—could reduce some of the anxious thoughts. I began to refer to these as *calming factors*.

When we understand dying as something that takes place in a community context, we need to consider those around us who are "influencers"—for good or for bad. Who in our *circle of influence* contributes to our stress? How do they affect the family as a whole? How do they interact with the person who is dying?

Monitoring anxiety is important and questions need to be asked about the source of that anxiety:

1. How do you think your family members are managing your dying?

This question invites conversation about family members and their response to what is going on. Are they okay? How are they doing? We worry about them and as such feel stress or anxiety because of how they are managing their journey.

2. Do you feel that your personal needs are being addressed?

If you are not feeling that you are being supported adequately, your stress level will rise and contribute to your overall anxiety about your circumstances. Sometimes the very people you believed would be there for you aren't and that raises the stress barometer.

3. Will you have someone present during your last hours or will you be alone when you die?

Most people do not want to die alone. They prefer someone is near them in their last hours. If people fear abandonment during their final hours, it can lead to anxiety. *Who will be there for me? Can I be certain I will not be left alone?*

4. Do you have any questions about your body shutting down?

This question is an important one. What will it look like? Will I die painfully or slowly? What can I expect? Uncertainty about pain management down the road can lead to anxiety in the present.

5. Do you have a question about where you are going to die?

People reflect on the location of their final moments on this earth. If they are at home, will they die there? If not, will they be taken to a hospice? Which one and what does it provide? *Will I die in a long-term care center, a hospital, at home or in a hospice?*

6. Do you have any concerns about the afterlife or believe there is one?

Many people begin to search for something bigger than themselves as they approach death, wondering if there might be something next. Some people are afraid of the idea of a God and wonder if they have disappointed God in some way. Is there a heaven? If there is, what's it like? If there is a God, is he kind or full of wrath? How can I know?

Or will I simply be reincarnated? Or just disappear back into dust? What happens to a person's soul? Maybe you've already asked these questions and found some answers, but some people are afraid to discuss these topics because there is so much variance of opinion.

The other factors that contribute to death anxiety are:

Unresolved Relationships

Whether it be someone you have not seen for a long time or a person who has impacted you negatively in the past, people who are dying begin to examine past difficult relationships. This creates stress for some people who need resolution.

Death Perception from Past Experiences

We don't always realize where our perception surrounding death develops, but subconscious images about death and dying—whether from one's personal family experience, from media or imagery—form our understanding. Anxiety can be produced by information that is faulty or misinterpreted.

Interference from the Outside

Many of us have encountered the rise of anxiety levels when a certain individual enters the room of the person who is ill and dying. This person creates anxiety just by being there—it may be their words, the way they engage or just their attitude. This person creates stress unintentionally, but very effectively. You may have to put boundaries on their contact with the dying person.

Unfiltered Information

In this technological world, where information on any subject can be found by entering a few key words into a search engine, we need to recognize the role and effect access to all this information has on our psyche—information that may not be accurate or helpful. We are searching for information in hopes of understanding what will happen to us in the future. On occasion, I've asked family members to give the Internet a break — information can be conflicting and erroneous.

Suffering and Pain

Much anxiety is a result of the unknown about a body slowing down and fear that the process might be unbearable. Resilience differs for each person. The ongoing promise to keep the patient updated and to continue to assure them that their pain will be managed effectively brings a sense of peace to an anxious heart.

Afterlife

Many people find comfort and peace in the notion that death isn't the end of their existence as a unique person — that their soul continues to live. Anxiety levels increase when people impose their own worldview on others. It is my experience with the dying that most people find comfort in an afterlife.

For those who are companioning the dying, we must always remember that we are not here to fix people. We journey with them as companions, either professionally, as family members or as friends. Learning to recognize some of the factors that are contributing to a loved one's stress or anxiety is one of the best gifts we can give them.

The above anxiety factors are important to know. Knowing about them has helped me engage people in meaningful conversations. I have also learned an enormous amount from these interactions and the people who were willing to talk through their anxiety with me. So talk. Converse. Share your fears. Listen to others. Be discerning as well.

Pam spent a lot of time reading her Bible, meditating on Bible verses she found helpful and just hanging out with her Lord. This gave her peace in her times of anxiety. It was her go-to method for keeping away what tried to keep her away from a peaceful passing.

Those who practice meditation or mindfulness are also able to manage anxiety better. Learn what works for you and put it into place in your daily routine.

When anxiety comes, know what you will do.

CHAPTER 14
Suffering — The Whole-Person Perspective

*We must learn to regard people less in the
light of what they do or omit to do, and
more in the light of what they suffer.*

– DIETRICH BONHOEFFER

Suffering can be an agent that brings us closer to ourselves, others and that which is holy.

Pam gave great back rubs, as well as incredible foot rubs. She had these amazing fingers. She was only 5'4" and had a small frame—but man, were her fingers strong! Whether it was on college choir tour with her peers or on her own children following a day on the ski slopes, she had golden hands that knew how to relieve muscle pain. The line-up for one of Pam's famous backrubs was constant and long. And she was always willing to oblige.

Toward the end of her illness, Pam's legs began to swell—it was quite painful for her, as the blood didn't flow quickly enough to where it needed to go. So we would massage her legs—each family member and her friends, too. Pam could not massage her own legs or feet. She would probably have done a better job than we did, but we all took turns getting the blood flowing. And as we did, we talked, shared, laughed... and probably cried inside as well.

Pam was on a steady diet of pills to manage her pain. We did our best to alleviate the pain based on our consultation with her medical team, but it was still hard for us to see her going through physical suffering. Pills, tubes, and needles — they were all laid out on her bedside table, ready to be administered according to schedule.

I learned a lot from my dying wife about whole-person suffering. I did not realize that suffering could take so many forms. Nor did I understand how I could either be a contributing factor to Pam's suffering or help lighten it. I discovered what a narrow view of end-of-life suffering I had — I really only considered physical suffering prior to Pam's illness.

Let's face it, death involves suffering of one sort or another. But what if we met suffering with the expectation that it could build intimacy, bring healing and restore relationships? Immediately you are thinking, "How could suffering possibly have anything good to contribute? How could anything positive come from it?"

Family members don't like to watch their loved ones suffer, so sometimes they distance themselves because they don't like to be reminded of their own mortality and they feel helpless in the face of another's suffering. I don't know how many times I have heard people say to me, "I'm not going to see Dad at the hospital because it's too hard for me." "I'm not taking the grandchildren down to see grandma in the hospice because I don't want that to be the last memory they have of her. I want them to remember Grandma before she got sick." Wait a second, who's afraid of suffering here? And who is teaching whom about the reality of suffering in life and how to relate with compassion to a person who is suffering?

Suffering is a part of life and pretending that it isn't just cuts off the possibility of learning about ourselves and what it is to be human. This is so important: if you don't lean into suffering and invite others to be a part of it, then you aren't seeing the bigger picture. Suffering must include others — we are built for community.

Physical suffering is not the only type of suffering. Whole-person suffering recognizes that even though we may be suffering in different parts of our life, other areas might actually be strong, healthy and vibrant. This vibrancy may lead to a final chapter of life that is full, meaningful and also filled with unexpected joy. It could lead to interactions and conversations that impact our lives and those closest to us forever.

And the amazing by-product of suffering is often intimacy. At least that's what began to happen in our family.

There was an invitation into intimacy during Pam's pain and suffering that was beautiful. There was a tender exchange because of Pam's total vulnerability. There was an openness to allow Pam to teach us as we engaged her at a level we had not experienced before, because we had never gone through dying.

As our body begins to fade, we struggle to come to grips with reality. We feel apprehensive as we see the visible signs of illness and mortality. We begin to look at ourselves differently and resist accepting the person we see in the mirror as our physical appearance changes. People leave the room and think, "She has changed so much since I last saw her." "I hardly recognized Dad. He's skin and bones." Have you ever thought that as you've said a final goodbye to a loved one?

Pam's body was continuing to shut down because of her cancer. We noticed the changes — and so did she. We gave her a gift one day. It was a picture frame with rotating digital photos of her and her family over the years. It sat next to her on the bedside table. She could look at the hundreds of photos and remember when she was younger, vibrant and healthy.

This was important for Pam — not because she was in any way vain, but because it reminded her of who she was. She knew she looked different now. But the outside is only one part of who we are. What areas of my life are healthy, vibrant, growing and even new? This is a crucial question in whole-person suffering.

When a person suffers, they do so from different parts of themselves. We are complex. We are created with heart, mind, body and soul. We may be strong in one area but suffering in another. As relational beings, we are called to help bear each other's burdens. If someone is suffering physically, we may not be able to remove the physical pain, but we can help alleviate that suffering by being present in other ways: relationally, emotionally, spiritually, mentally. Every area of our life influences the other. Each area impacts the other.

Do not underestimate the impact you have, as a community, on whole-person suffering by spending time with a family member who is dying.

Some people will appear strong and physically fit, but have a debilitating emotional challenge. That's suffering. Some people have a body that is deteriorating due to illness, but have an inner strength that is uncanny. I have counseled many people with a variety of problems. I always try to help them determine what areas of their life they feel are the most vibrant and strong before we tackle the suffering they are experiencing. Many find this approach empowering because it expands personhood beyond a physical body or external appearance to a much more holistic approach that is conducive to healing and empowerment. Yes, we may not be healed from our physical challenges, but acknowledging areas that are still vibrant in us is significant for a peaceful passing.

I have not had cancer. I don't know the physical pain of experiencing tumors growing in my body—I pray I never do. But Pam did. Her mantra was always, "I do not have to suffer alone. I have my family, my friends, my church community and I have God." She invited us to participate in her suffering as much as she could. It was a privilege, because we watched her courage in the midst of it.

Let's consider suffering from a whole-person perspective. What kinds of suffering should we be aware of during those final days on earth?

Physical Suffering

Physical suffering is the most obvious type of suffering because others can see it—it's more material. You have heard the term "pain level" or "pain tolerance." Medical professionals will ask, "On a scale between 1 and 10, what is your pain level?" We honor the physical suffering of each individual without judgment.

Mental Suffering

Simply put, our brain is a delicate balance of chemistry, neural pathways and connections. When any of these are out of whack, we experience suffering and process information that comes into our lives in ways that aren't helpful.

Spiritual Suffering

Deep anger and despair toward God represent a unique suffering that leaves us feeling detached from a higher power and from something bigger than ourselves. Our soul searches for light in the midst of darkness and our hearts harden as we make ourselves the center of our own universe.

Emotional Suffering

Reoccurring negative emotions (like anger, guilt and self-hatred) that leave us exhausted and at odds with ourselves and others can drive us into depression. Who knew that the beloved Robin Williams who warmed our hearts and made the world laugh was crying inside?

Relational Suffering

People suffer because of relationships that are no longer there or are toxic, unhealthy or abusive. If a person does not recognize and come to terms with this suffering (and perhaps set healthy boundaries), they continue to live with an unhealed wound that impacts their life and the lives of those around them.

Suffering from Purposelessness

"Why am I here?" "What is my purpose?" "What makes my life and contribution to this world significant?" When someone suffers from a loss of identity and purpose in life, they lose sight of all the possibilities in their life.

Suffering Past Losses

Many people do not recognize this deep suffering because it's so hidden and can masquerade as other issues. We can suffer from something that was taken away from us unexpectedly and has not been grieved or processed in a healthy and productive manner.

If you take a few moments to examine what areas of a person's life are healthy and in which areas they are experiencing suffering, you might be surprised by what you find. You might be even more surprised to discover your possible positive or negative contribution to that person's suffering!

Interactions are important. What can I bring to help the person dying live life the best they can during their final days on earth?

- The words I say (or don't say)
- The information that I provide can be helpful (or not)
- My presence (or my absence)
- My affirmation of their purpose (or lack of affirmation)
- My ability to listen to their deeper questions (or ignore them)

- My ability to acknowledge difficult feelings (or quickly change the topic)

Each day I would notice physical changes in Pam's body. As she became thinner, her bones began to protrude more and more. Her abdomen continued to swell and required ongoing draining because of the disease that was still actively growing and wreaking havoc on her major organs. We rubbed her legs to increase circulation. "That feels so good," she would say, even though her legs felt like sponges to our touch. And we knew she was still in physical discomfort despite our attempts to alleviate the swelling.

This is to be expected when your body is not well. You have very little control over a body that's fighting to keep you physically alive. But you can make choices that allow you to live life fully in other areas of life until your last breath.

The last photo of Pam was taken outdoors 13 days before she died and holds a very special memory for me. Pam's sister Carol Ann and her husband Scott were helping care for Pam since I had to be away at church preaching that morning.

Pam wanted to take a ride in the country in their new convertible. Because she was too weak to get out of bed, Scott picked up this beautiful and now very fragile woman and carried her to the convertible and placed her carefully in the front seat. With a blanket wrapped around her for warmth, a bright aqua blue hat on her head, and a smile on her face, Pam was delighted to take a ride out in the country. It would be her last one.

Carol Ann told me later it was a beautiful experience. As the wind gently brushed against her face, Pam began to lead the others in songs of praise to God—a trio of singers, laughing and enjoying one more day together. Pam knew that her days were numbered but chose life instead.

Beware of attributing the word *suffering* just to the physical. We might be suffering in multiple areas in our lives or not, but operating out of our areas of strength helps us compensate for those areas where we are suffering and keeps us moving forward.

As Pam began to get weaker, her major organs started to shut down. We administered the pain medication on schedule to try to keep her as pain-free as possible. But there were many nights when Pam would wake me up and ask if I could read to her. She had a small book of comforting Bible verses and I would take it out and read to her from that. I would pray for her. It brought her comfort.

I could not bear Pam's physical suffering but I could be present in other ways. We sang to her, we touched her and we held her close. She held a small wooden cross in her hand as she fell asleep for the evening. We told her we were proud of her. We spoke words of love and let her know we would be close by her no matter what and that if she fell asleep she could count on us to be there when she opened her eyes again.

Intimacy happens without expecting anything in return. I just wanted to be a good husband. I wanted to help my wife. I wanted her to live. I wanted to alleviate whatever suffering she was experiencing in her whole being at a given time.

I did not realize what was being given to me in those moments of pain and suffering as I heard the frail voice of my wife saying, "Thank you, Rick." I wondered how much longer I would hear Pam's voice speak my name out loud. I couldn't understand how I could fall deeper in love with someone as they neared death, but I did. I really did.

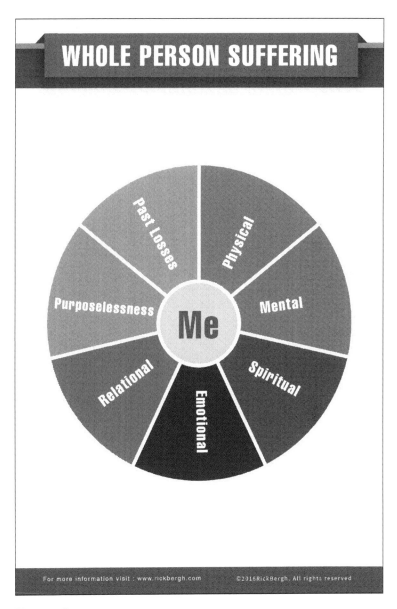

WHOLE PERSON SUFFERING

Past Losses

Physical

Purposelessness

Me

Mental

Relational

Emotional

Spiritual

Figure 3

CHAPTER 15
Only You
Know When You
Are Ready

Since you will carry your soul
into eternity, it's worth checking up
on at least as often as your teeth.

– JOHN ORTBERG

N obody likes to be told that they are "giving up" on life. Nobody likes to be told that it is "okay to let go." Neither response is helpful.

I like to suggest to people when they are dying that they take time to go in and discover what's appropriate for them. What do I mean by *go in*?

There is an internal conversation that takes place inside the psyche of someone who is dying. As onlookers, we want to be privy to it, but I'm not convinced it's ours to hear. This conversation revolves around the question: "Is it my time?"

It's a very personal and existential question almost every single person I have cared for eventually asks along the journey. *Is it time to put the pen down and let another become the journalist for the rest of my story?*

You will know when it's time to let go. Some people fight to the very end and believe they will defeat death know matter what. Most people are able to accept the outcome of their disease and come to terms with the inevitable based on their prognosis. It differs for each of us.

June was dying. She was the mom of three children and only in her 40's. She had breast cancer. I was officiating at another funeral when June's husband, Larry, showed up and was looking at me from the back of the hall. He seemed very anxious. I thought June had died from the expression on his face.

I finished the service and went back to speak to Larry. He said, "June wants to let go but she doesn't know how to. Could you please come?" "Of course," I said. "I will come as soon as I can." Larry was distraught and I knew I would have to make my way over to the hospital as quickly as possible. I skipped the lunch at the wake and arrived at the local hospital. There was no hospice in this small town.

June was tired. She had been fighting this awful disease for a number of months. She had done all she could. She had fought hard. "Tell me what's going on in your heart," I said. "I don't know how to die, but it's time," she answered. We talked about what could be holding her back and concluded that she was having difficulty telling her three children that it was her time to die.

I went to speak with her children, two girls and a boy, all under the age of 16. We spoke about their feelings, what was happening inside their hearts. We spoke about their understanding of the afterlife and what happens when someone dies. And then I said, "Your mom really wants to talk to you about the next step in her life. I would like each of you to go in and see your mom." June had the tough conversation with each of her children. It was hard, but she said, "I need to go to heaven now. I don't want to leave you but I have to. Remember that we can see each other again. I love you so much." They told me later that those were her final words to each of them.

We assume that letting go is a kind of metaphysical crap-shoot—just a non-verbal experience. But I would disagree—it's an intentional release. Letting go is a significant conversation between two people who are able to cut the line between them, while still believing there is a new line to attach to. June discovered that and died a few days later.

Death and a final letting go cannot be forced. I have heard people say to their loved ones, "It's okay to let go now," thinking they were being helpful. And I wondered to myself when I heard that, "Do they really have the right to say those words?" People know when it's the right time. You need to be prepared to accept it in their time and when it's offered to you. Your words may push them away before they are ready to leave. This request that they "let go" may be more about meeting your needs than theirs—as harsh as that sounds.

We sat at the kitchen table, each of us believing and hoping that Pam could still get better. We made her favorite food, hoping she would eat and get stronger. She needed to gain strength. We were doing everything possible to give her a chance to keep on fighting the cancer. We kept believing, hoping and praying.

And then one night she pushed her plate away. "I don't want to eat any more," she said. "It's not enjoyable for me anymore," she continued. She said this in a very firm voice that was uncharacteristic of Pam—so we knew we had to listen to what she was saying to all of us. We heard it clearly and needed to honor her request. That was not easy. You die if you stop eating. But her body was no longer able to digest food. It was rejecting it. She was preparing for her final days on this earth. We sat back for a few moments. "Okay, Mom," we said. She smiled and said, "Thank you." Later that night, once I was alone, I cried in my office.

The next day I approached Pam in our bedroom as she lay listening to a CD of hymns her parents had given her. "How can you let go now? I don't want you to give up. Why now?" I begged. "What is different than before?" I pushed her for an answer. She looked at me and said, "Rick, I can let go because I know the faith of my children. I will see them again," she said simply. I cried again and she held me in her arms.

She didn't give up—she went in. Her faith and hope in another place beyond this earth allowed her to believe she really would see her kids again and enabled her to let go of them.

After having cancer take away her healthy body for five straight years, she deserved something better. It was only right to honor her request, as difficult as it was. We did. And that day she called each of her children into her room and asked them to let go and to trust God and his plan for her and for them.

Of course we prayed for a miracle. Every day. But we were all doing our best to begin the process of honoring her end-of-life wishes. She was doing her best to begin to release us. She was trusting in a bigger and higher power she knew as God to take over what would be her next story as she completed this one on earth.

This is an extremely difficult transition for family members. You want to live in hope because you just never know—there have been people the entire medical profession has given up on and, for some crazy reason, suddenly recover from a terminal disease. This does happen and it may happen for some of you as well.

One dying man said to me, "I'm starting to see a clarity in my life I have never seen before." "Can you tell me more?" I asked. "I've had lots of time to think. I've actually talked to God more in the last two weeks than I have my entire life," he continued. "May I ask you what you talked to God about?" I said. "Well, at first it was me just yelling at him—*I don't want this cancer; I don't think I deserve to have it*—I didn't know who else to express my feelings to. I didn't want to be angry with my wife, my children or the doctors. That wouldn't be fair. So I screamed at God from inside myself. Then we kind of just talked back and forth. I guess I kind of made my peace with him," he admitted. "I was thinking back to my grandma and what she said about God when I was a kid growing up and it helped me to think about what was next—it encouraged me," he continued.

This man went inside and discovered a treasure that helped him die peacefully.

When people begin to have a conversation with God, they connect with the Holy. That's the inner world of the soul and it's a mystery. Even those who already appear to have a strong relationship with God prior to their terminal prognosis seem to experience something even deeper with the sacred during an illness and as they approach death.

This was true for Pam. Even though her body was slowly turning to skin and bones, her heart became a window into her soul. I could not wait to ask, hear and listen to what was happening deep inside her heart. The wisdom, insight and love I experienced from Pam were amazing.

I couldn't help but think that Pam had a connection with God I had not experienced before—and wouldn't unless someday I'm in a similar predicament as she was. If God is all about bringing people together after death, then why wouldn't he come closer to Pam to get ready for this event? If God was in fact drawing closer to Pam as she drew closer to death, I wanted to be attuned to the "conversations" they were having.

Jesus' disciples in the Bible were having trouble with the fact that he was going to die and leave them. They didn't want to believe it to be true. He said to them, "Do not let your hearts be troubled. You believe in God, believe also in me. My Father's house has many rooms; if that were not so, would I have told you that I am going there to prepare a place for you? And if I go and prepare a place for you, I will come back and take you to be with me that you also may be where I am." (John 14: 1-3, NIV)

I'm not suggesting everyone has the same worldview as our family. You will decide for yourself what you believe about death and what your understanding is of what is next is for you. It is my narrative research with hundreds of people, not only at end of life but during funerals and memorial services, that made me conclude that people need assurance of what's next. Of the hundreds of funerals I've been involved with, there were only a few that did not include in some way the hope of heaven, eternal life, or the hereafter in their eulogies. Listen to what people say the next time you attend a funeral.

Martin Luther said, "Every man must do two things alone; he must do his own believing and his own dying." Although I believe dying is a communal event, I think Luther might have been referring to that free fall of going in and letting go. This is the part of dying that is yours alone, to go in and discover for yourself. It cannot be forced on you.

For our family, there was and still is an amazing peace that allows us to release our lives and our family's lives to a God who loves and promises to provide a new place for us to go. I know not everyone has the same faith or belief system, but all I can say from being with people of every religious background or spiritual flavor when dying, *hope* is the number one peace giver and *hope* does not come from people when you are dying. We can only experience this hope from somewhere else and this hope can exist and does exist in our soul—where we can meet the sacred. It's in the soul where the wrestling match of questions takes place and we are finally able to release what we ultimately have no control over.

Going in for Pam allowed her to let go and let God take over the final paragraphs of her life story.

Soul work is done when people want to come to some conclusions about God and the afterlife—questions stir...

- Are you real, God?
- Will you be with me in my suffering?
- Will death cut me off from you, God?
- Will you forgive me?
- Do I need to reconcile any of my life's choices or get right with people?
- Will you be there at my death?
- What will it look like when my soul leaves my body?
- Is there really a heaven?

Fear of the unknown can hold large portions of our emotional and mental life hostage. We may not admit this freely and much of this might not easily be expressed if it has been foreign to us in the past. But you can't live freely when you live in angst.

Your understanding of hope may be different than mine, and you will need to come to terms with how this will impact your life. I'm only here to tell you my story and share my experience and invite you to remove obstacles in your life that may get in the way of your happiness and joy.

In the movie *Gravity*, we see an astronaut, Dr. Stone [played by Sandra Bullock], struggling to look beyond the traumatic death of her only child—a daughter killed in an accident. The movie takes us through a number of turbulent scenes that resonate with the internal grief she is experiencing. They finally bring her face to face with her deep missing of her daughter.

It looks as if she is not going to be able to return to earth as a result of a mechanical problem on her space shuttle. All the other crew members have died. She is the only one remaining, separated from earth and all communication. She is alone in her thoughts and feelings as she is faced with her own impending death. She resolves to finally give up and contemplates death by suicide. She decides to remove the oxygen flow in the cabin and die. Then the movie takes a profound turn.

She begins to ask questions out loud. While she knows death is a reality for everyone, she is still scared. She wonders if anyone will think of her once she is gone, if anyone is praying for her and she wishes that someone had taught her to pray.

She thinks of her child again and then turns off the oxygen supply. As she begins to lose consciousness. Kowalski (her fellow astronaut who had died) mysteriously enters the capsule. He has a conversation with her in which he challenges her to continue living, and not to give up on life. This dialogue causes her to change her mind and she turns back on the oxygen supply.

She asks Kowalski to say "hi" to her daughter on her behalf, realizing that Kowalski has died and is on his way to something beyond—she had seen him float off into space and knew he was dead. But her words to him indicate that she believes that he is going where her daughter has also gone.

She tells him to give her a big kiss and to tell her that Mom misses her. She has a certainty of something beyond that gives her assurance to live on. There is a hope that they can be together again. There is something beyond this life.

I am not telling you what to believe. All I know is that I believe there is a place beyond earth, which I call heaven, and it is where my previous wife has gone and where we can meet again.

Pam and I both shared that hope.

CHAPTER 16

Near-Death Surprises That Will Have You Marveling

*Our inability to see the beauty
doesn't suggest in the slightest that
beauty is not there. Rather, it suggests
that we are not looking carefully enough
or with broad enough perspective
to see the beauty.*

– RABBI HAROLD KUSHNER

You should never underestimate the importance of near-death awareness experiences. It's not our job to discern whether or not they are real. The logical mind is rarely willing to accept what it can't see or touch. Near-death experiences are beyond what we can wrap our heads around so we tend to dismiss them as nonsense or hallucinations due to chemical changes.

Whether we call them visions, dreams or spiritual encounters is not the issue. The question is whether they are helpful to the one dying.

After experiencing so many people on their deathbed, I have come to believe that the veil is thin. Watch carefully when people die. You'll learn a lot. I know I did.

About a week before Pam died, I was out of the house, but her sister Carol Ann was present.

"Carol Ann!" Pam shouted to her sister. "Come here!" she said. "I need you to get me a pen and paper! Right now!" she insisted. Carol Ann, a little surprised, listened and promptly returned to Pam's room.

"Okay, write down these names," she said to her sister. "What do you want me to write down?" Carol Ann asked. "A list of people I want to meet in heaven," Pam continued. Carol Ann was surprised by Pam's assertive attitude. She was serious and no nonsense. "I need you to write this list right away," she continued. So Carol Ann started writing.

The list included her grandma and grandpa, my father and grandma, her special friend, Pat, and a few others. And then she concluded by saying, "And put Moses on that list, too. I have some questions to ask him." Carol Ann meticulously wrote each name and Pam went to sleep. We still have that list.

What was that about? Pam was serious. We took her seriously. What was she saying to us? She was obviously preparing for her next journey with hope and expectation. This encouraged us greatly, knowing she believed so strongly in an afterlife, and that she was preparing for her next conversations with people she knew and loved and a few others beside. Hallucinations? Dreams?

Yes, we knew Pam was drawing closer to her death and we began to see how she was preparing.

A couple of weeks before Pam died, she woke me up in the middle of the night and asked me to turn the light off. "But Pam, there's no light on," I said to her. "Yes, there is," Pam said. "I think it's the bathroom light," she continued, pointing toward that corner of the room. There was no light on — the room was pitch black. "It's not that bright," she said, "but it woke me up — it's not good to leave any lights on, Rick," she said to me. Pam was very lucid as she spoke. It dawned on me that she was seeing something I was not. Was I standing on holy ground?

I got up and pretended to go toward the bathroom to turn off the light. "Thanks," she said and went back to sleep.

I lay awake for quite some time thinking about what had just happened. I don't know what it's like to die, but it made me wonder if when we are close to death, God comes closer to us incrementally. How he comes is a mystery, but I wondered if in some way I was experiencing a transcendent God rending the veil to draw closer to one of his children.

Three nights later Pam woke me up again and asked me again to turn off the light. "Is it bothering you?" I asked. "No it's not bothering me," she replied. "I'm just wondering if it is keeping you awake?" she continued. "It's not super bright," she said. "But it's like I can reach out and touch it," she said. I was amazed. "I will get the light, Pam," I said. "Thanks, honey," she said and went back to sleep.

She was drawing close to death. In some ways, I wanted to see what she was seeing. It left me speechless and amazed — the thought of an all powerful, yet intimate, creative being drawing close to Pam made me cry both inside and out. I was face to face with the reality of what I was going to miss, but also what Pam was going to experience because of God's amazing grace and love for her.

I have experienced so many of these moments in my life — when God seems a breath away. I yearn to be present for them and take in their spiritual significance. They have encouraged me in my doubting and challenged me in my believing. Those experiences when the mysterious and the holy touches earth.

A nurse phoned me and asked if I could be with a lady who was dying. She was alone. She had no family close by. "It would be nice if someone could come and sit with her," she said. "I will be right down," I replied. It was a rural hospital so there was no designated room for the dying, but it was a room with a single bed for some privacy.

As I arrived, I immediately became disappointed because the lady had slipped into unconsciousness and I was unable to have a conversation with her. I don't know what got into me, but I decided to sing—just simple songs. I would sing softly. They were just simple children's songs that I learned when I was in Sunday school. As I sang, I held her hand. I looked at her. I stroked her forehead lightly. "I wish her family were here," I said to myself. I kept on singing.

When I ran out of songs I started in on *Jesus Loves Me* and before I had finished the first verse, this old, wrinkled, dying, beautiful woman opened her eyes fully. She looked up toward the ceiling. She raised her hands toward the ceiling as high as she could. She smiled—eyes wide open—brought her arms down, crossed them over her chest and breathed her last breath. I sat there in awe. I cannot describe the feeling in that room in those final moments. It was warm. It was peaceful. It was powerful. I was moved to tears. It was such an honor to share that moment with this amazing woman and see her ushered into what was next. I marveled. To know that her family missed out on this amazing experience made me sad.

Don't let your understanding of spirituality limit you from being open to experiencing moments at the end of life that are not easily explained. These may well be final gifts you are privileged to receive if you are open and willing. So be careful not to treat them lightly or diminish their significance.

Pam loved to sing and we had a stereo set up in her room. She had a gift with music and a wonderful way with children. She had directed many choirs in her lifetime—she had a children's choir in nearly every church where we served. Music was definitely her way to connect with God, her spiritual pathway.

Pam was on some pretty heavy drugs to manage her pain level and, during the last few days, was in and out of conversation with us. There were long periods of time when her eyes were not open and we were just present with her. We sat beside her. Massaged her legs. Moistened her mouth. Placed lip balm on her lips. Not often, but once in a while, she would open her eyes. We would gaze into them. We kept on telling her that we loved her over and over again. She would try to say the words back — but would smile instead.

We knew Pam loved music, so one night all of us who were in the house at the time decided to gather around her bed to sing. They were all songs of our childhood and hymns from our faith background. We began to sing and enjoy the spirit of music as it filled the room. What we were not expecting was this…every time we couldn't remember the words of a particular verse, Pam would chime in and sing it, filling in the blanks. She remembered every word. And then we noticed that one word she shouted out even louder than any of the others was "JESUS!" She was connecting to God at a level that was beyond our comprehension. It was a very powerful experience for all of us. We felt God's presence in a way we knew was not humanly possible.

Scott, our brother-in-law, expressed it well when he said, "The Spirit is thick in here tonight." And it was.

To be present with a person in their final hours is an honor. It's a sacred time not to be taken lightly nor passed off as insignificant. I often encourage people to listen carefully, to be open to what might be bigger than them and to look for the peace that may come in the last hours.

CHAPTER 17
It's Never Too Late For One Last View

When I took the leap, I had faith I would find a net; Instead I learned I could fly.

– JOHN CALVIN

When I was younger, I was in a hurry and needed to get to a hockey game because I was the goalie. In my haste, I used the wrong contact solution and burnt my eyes very badly. It was the cleaning solution I had used and not the saline. Talk about painful. I played the game but I didn't play well. Following the hockey game, I returned home, seeing very imperfectly. I did not know what was happening.

By one in the morning, I couldn't stand the pain any longer so I went to the hospital. They froze my eyes, and applied secure patches to my eyes that would need to be left on for 48 hours. "Don't remove them and don't let any light get in there. We will see if they are okay when you open your eyes."

That was a long 48 hours for me. I was wondering if I had done long-term damage. I was scared I would never see again.

Pam was so sick, but I did not want her to close her eyes — I never knew if I would get to look into them again. It was nighttime. Everyone was going to sleep. We had spent the day with Pam, had sung with her and had told her we loved her. We said goodnight and hoped we would talk to her again in the morning. I stayed with Pam. She slept next to me as I took care of her. She was so tired. We were all tired. She needed to die and she knew it. Even we knew it, so we waited. And we all wondered how much longer she would live, even though we did not say it out loud. Would this be her last night alive? Would she make it through the night? Would we see her in the morning?

Pam was ready to go to sleep and wake up in heaven. I think it was tiring for her to see her family in front of her, knowing she would not be able to see them again this side of heaven. We all wanted her to live, but we knew how exhausted she was. We knew she was ready to go to heaven. She had told us so many times.

A couple of weeks earlier, she had called her mom into the room: "Come quickly, Mom!" she said. "What is it, Honey?" her mom asked. "This might be my greatest day ever," Pam said with exuberance. "Why?" her mom asked. "This might be the day I get to go to heaven," Pam exclaimed. They hugged and cried. Pam was such an optimist who prepared us well for the end of her story and gave us a window into what was next. She was seeing something very clearly from her vantage point and it inspired us all. I couldn't see what she was seeing, but I was inspired by her faith.

Those eyes. There was something beautiful about Pam's eyes. Looking deeply into them gave me insight into her soul. Don't eyes speak something to us that words can never communicate? How many times had I gazed deeply into Pam's eyes? I loved her so much.

It's amazing how every other part of your body can reveal decay, but your eyes speak right to the end. They reveal something deep inside.

You always want more time. There's never enough time. You want a few more moments and yet you know deep down there is a time for everything and that includes closing your eyes for the final time.

My last night with Pam was very difficult for me, as her husband. Everyone else had gone to bed. They had kissed her and said good-night to her even though she had not opened her eyes for a number of hours or spoken a word.

As Pam labored for air, and her body fought for life, I lay beside my wife, stroking her face.

I kissed her on the cheek often. I talked to her but she did not respond. Maybe she heard my words. I hope she did.

I told her I loved her, that she was so precious to me, and was such a great mother.

One of Pam's favorite TV show was *The Waltons*. So I decided I needed to turn on that program. It helped me as I thought about my life with Pam. It had been so good, so wonderful.

I said a lot of things to her that night, including that I was sorry to her for not being a better husband. She had told me I was a good husband many times. But I wondered if I could have been a better spouse and done anything differently.

I prayed hard that night, and believe me — God and I had some aggressive conversation going on. I became angry at him again and then begged him to perform a last-minute miracle.

I thought of my kids and wondered how they would manage without a mom. I begged God to take me instead. To let us switch places. They needed their mom more than they needed me, I told God. *Let me take her place. Please, Jesus, please.*

All night was like emotional whiplash, first begging God to let her die and the next moment imploring God to intervene and heal her. I thought about my life without Pam and remembered what she had said to me about moving forward with my life once she was gone.

I didn't want her to go and yet I did. *No more of this, God. Let her die and find peace.* I wondered if I needed the peace more than she did. She seemed at peace with God already, but I was struggling to find any meaning in this death. Still.

And yet, the peace I felt in that room was something I can't describe. I had experienced it before with others at the end of their lives, but it was different for me now as I prepared to say goodbye to my wife.

While I was extremely sad, I was also hopeful at the same time. I knew with full confidence this would not be the last time I would see Pam, but I wished we could have had more time together as husband and wife.

Death has a physical odor — I knew Pam's body was coming to its last moments. I had been with many in this scenario and knew all the signs. My lifetime of memories with her flashed in front of me, as I reflected on our 25 years together. I also thought about what I would miss most until we meet again beyond this life on earth.

At 7:15 in the morning, Carol Ann and Scott came back into the room. Pam had made it through the night. "We should maybe reposition her," I said. "Let's put her on her other side," Carol Ann said. So we did — and then we were amazed at what happened next.

Could this be the miracle we were hoping for?

Pam opened her eyes. She lifted herself up. "Pam!" we said, looking into her eyes, hearts beating. I had never ever seen Pam's eyes so blue. So big. So inviting. It was hard to explain. "Pam!" I said, trying to look into her eyes. I wanted her to see me one more time. I wanted her to see me — but she was not looking at me, or Scott or Carol Ann. She was looking ahead to something beyond us. She was looking beyond this world. Pam smiled brightly. She lay back on her pillow and breathed her last breath. The end of her story on earth was beautiful, hopeful. Her concluding paragraph, amazing.

Wow! I thought to myself. *She's alive again. She has a new life. Till death do us part.* And then I cried. I was so happy I had looked into Pam's eyes that one last time. It didn't matter that she wasn't looking at me because what she was looking at would join us all together again.

I went and told each of the children that their mom had died. Each came to the bedside of their mom. I gave them time. It was hard. It had been a hard five years since Pam was first diagnosed with cancer.

Other family members came and cried, too. We talked about Pam and the hope we had as a family to place her in the hands of God who immediately gave her new life and the first new breath she would experience in paradise.

We were happy for her but sad for us.

Now we would have to learn what it would be like to live life without Pam. We needed to step into a life that would not include her physical presence in our ongoing stories.

I was not certain what that life would look like for us now. I wondered about tomorrow. I really didn't want to even think about the next day or the days to follow. I just cried when I thought about my life without Pam.

I was scared to close my eyes that first night without her there. Why? I knew I would have to open them again in the morning and it would be the first time in 25 years that I would not see my wife lying next to me.

A life without Pam.

In all honesty, I wanted to close my eyes to the future. I did not want to think about the next chapter of my life without her in it.

A life without Pam.

Didn't choose it.

Didn't want it.

Didn't want to think about it.

The next morning came. I opened my eyes. I flung my arm across our bed to touch my wife, as I had done for 25 years. Then the realization hit me hard. I was alone. I was by myself. Pam was gone. I cried hard into my pillow.

That day I began the next chapter of my life and wondered what would be next.

It was hard for me to pick up my pen and write.

But I did.

About the Author

Rick Bergh, author of *Finding Anchors, Taking Notice* and *Cancer Diagnosis*, was born and raised in Alberta, Canada, and educated at Augustana University College, University of Alberta, and Saskatoon Lutheran Theological Seminary.

When Rick was 49 years of age, his life took a dramatic turn when his wife Pam (age 47) died of ovarian cancer. It set him and his four children on a transitional journey of loss.

This journey forced him to dig more deeply into his own story as he entered a new chapter in his life.

In the process, it became apparent to him that he was being prepared for something new. He stepped out into this new arena, trusting and believing in his next chapter. Setting aside a full-time career as an ordained Lutheran minister, he immersed himself in the study of death, dying and bereavement (Thanatology), adding his own family's experience with cancer as the touchstone of his work.

He is a Certified Thanatologist (CT), a designation bestowed by the Association for Death Education and Counseling (ADEC) after rigorous study in the area of death, dying and grief. In addition to his counseling practice, Rick is an author and speaker and has been heard numerous times on national radio in Canada.

Rick strongly believes in the importance of narrative in our lives. In his books you will find stories from his own personal life and those with whom he has worked throughout his professional career. Rick's method of counseling includes Narrative Therapy, which he has studied and applied to his ongoing work as an educator, speaker and author.

Rick's 30-year vocation as a parish pastor positioned him among people who were continually trying to adapt to unexpected transitions. His practical approach to transitional loss is a result of hundreds of hours spent with individuals who were working through their loss as individuals or as a family.

His many years of work in the community as a volunteer, sports coach, community counselor, educator and funeral officiant has broadened his knowledge and experience as he engaged people in their everyday challenges—listening and learning from their powerful stories.

His career change from pastor to businessman afforded him the opportunity to travel the world, expanding his awareness of cultural differences and universal truths in the area of loss.

You can connect with Rick on his popular blogging website (www.intentionalgrief.com) where he shares his thoughts, stories and resources of practical approaches to loss. You can also check out his many other resources at www.rickbergh.com.

Rick Bergh and his wife Erica currently live in Cochrane, Alberta, Canada, in the foothills of the Rocky Mountains.

Taking "Looking Ahead" to the Next Level

As part of his ongoing purpose to engage people in conversation about the end of life and its deeper significance, Rick offers a number of keynote speeches, talks and workshops. Rick challenges our assumptions about illness, death and dying, moving his audiences to look at this topic through a different colored lens.

A Chapter Worth Writing — Keynote

Are you worried that your life will not have purpose as you face a life-limiting illness or terminal prognosis? This lecture speaks to anyone who has ever felt that the last chapter of their life holds little significance or purpose. Rick Bergh offers a framework for discerning what is essential, eliminating what is not essential, and removing obstacles that prevent your final days from having a lasting impact.

A Chapter Worth Writing will help you to pick up your pen and author your own story. Make the most of your minutes. Find new and ongoing purpose for your life. And invite your family and friends into your final days.

Dying as a Communal Initiative — Keynote

Is fear of the unknown holding you back from caring for your loved one who has a life-limiting illness? This lecture speaks to anyone who has ever felt they are ill-equipped to care for a family member at home in their final days. By challenging limiting beliefs about death and dying, Rick will create a framework for families and provide practical tools that will empower them to honor the end-of-life wishes of their loved one at home.

Applying "Looking Ahead" Principles—Leadership Development Training

What is most important as you approach your final chapter of life? In this workshop, Rick Bergh gives participants the tools for engaging families and patients during their final days on earth. Learn to eliminate what is not essential. Learn what is most important in facilitating end-of-life conversations between family members and the one dying that will lead to a peaceful passing and lasting positive memories.

You can learn more about Rick Bergh's speaking engagements at www.rickbergh.com or email him at rick@rickbergh.com.

Free Resources

Please go to www.rickbergh.com/lookingahead/charts to receive a free copy of the three charts found in the book and recommendations on how to use them effectively.

Figure 1 –
Circle of Influence
(Chapter 4)

Figure 2 –
When Building a
Team of Experts
Includes Family
(Chapter 8)

Figure 3 –
Suffering – The
Whole-Person
Perspective
(Chapter 14)

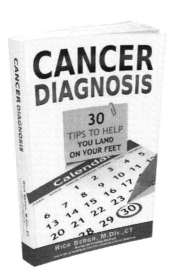

It's practical, it's realistic and it's smart!

If there is a concise and easy-to-read book to help you land on your feet after a cancer diagnosis, this is it.

Rick Bergh offers his readers 30 short lessons with action steps for those recently diagnosed with cancer and their family members and friends – one a day for 30 days.

Cancer Diagnosis: 30 Tips to Help You Land on Your Feet will give you:

- Hope to face the future
- Direction to empower your journey
- Education to move your forward
- Insight to make wise decisions

Far beyond a collection of good ideas, this book lays out 30 effective nuggets that bring results. Developed by Rick, a father of four, in his own personal journey with a wife who had cancer, his family courageously found ways to face their mom's diagnosis and inspire friends and family to be a part of their significant journey.

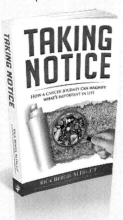
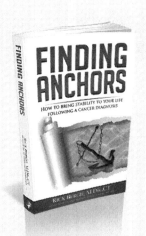

Made in the USA
Charleston, SC
30 December 2016